WHY ME?

WHY ME?

Harnessing
the Healing Power
of the Human Spirit

GARRETT PORTER &
PATRICIA A. NORRIS, PH.D.

Foreword by Gerald G. Jampolsky, M.D.

STILLPOINT PUBLISHING
WALPOLE, NEW HAMPSHIRE

FIRST PRINTING

This book is manufactured in the United States of
America. It has been typeset
by Batsch Co., Inc. and printed by
The Maple-Vail Book Manufacturing Group.
It is designed by James F. Brisson,
photos by Danilo Boschung/
Skyline Features, cover photo by
Timothy Forcade and published by Stillpoint
Publishing, Box 640, Meetinghouse Road,
Walpole, NH 03608.

Published simultaneously in Canada by
Fitzhenry & Whiteside Limited, Toronto.

Library of Congress Card Catalog Number: 84-52877
Why Me? Garrett Porter & Patricia A. Norris, Ph.D.
ISBN 0-913299-19-7

*This book is lovingly dedicated
to my parents, Elmer and Alyce Green,
who envisioned the Voluntary Control of Internal States
and have dedicated their lives to demonstrating
the value and practicality
of conscious self-regulation.*

—PAT NORRIS

*This book is dedicated to
Eric Bossey
and
Michele Peterson
and
Terry Oberdine,
my best friends,
and to their families
and mine.*

—GARRETT PORTER

NOTE TO THE READER

WHY ME? explains the logic of visualization and imagery as well as anything I have read. It can convince a cancer patient not only to try it but to believe it will work, in which case it *will* work. It should help a cancer patient who is dedicated to doing everything in their power to live. At the least, it will improve the quality of their life by demonstrating that there is always an option enabling them to get back in command of their life.

Dick Bloch

Co-founder of H&R Block

Table of Contents

FOREWORD

*G*arrett Porter is the experience of a lifetime. So are his parents and Dr. Patricia Norris.

Garrett and I first met on the telephone, and what immediately struck me was his zest and enthusiasm for life, his humor, his determined belief that the mind controls the body and not vice versa, and that in every way possible nothing is impossible.

And yet what impressed me the most was his heart filled with love and his eager desire to be of help to others. A born teacher is he. A miracle of love is he.

By his own initiative he started his own telephone network—really a love network—that was patterned after the national telephone network at our own Center for Attitudinal Healing in Tiburon, California.

When I met Garrett in person, just before he was to appear with me and other children on the NBC special,

"Donahue and Kids," he was everything and more than his letters and phone calls revealed.

It has been an absolute joy and delight to be a witness to Garrett's helping so many people, both professional and non-professional.

Dr. Norris is to be congratulated on her partnership of dual learning where each became teacher/student, student/teacher to each other.

WHY ME? is the remarkable story of how your own thoughts can change how you perceive the world and yourself. It is a story of hope and positive thinking that can change the life of everyone who reads this book.

—Gerald Jampolsky, M.D.

PREFACE

*T*his book began when I wanted to bring Garrett's story to my colleagues, so I wrote a paper, "The Role of Psychophysiologic Self-regulation in the Treatment of Cancer: a Narrative Case Report," to present at a conference. As is customary, I gave Garrett a pseudonym, and knowing his feelings of connectedness with his work, I asked him to choose the name I would use. He was indignant and tried to talk me into using his own name. When I explained that it would be very unorthodox and I would not be comfortable doing it, he chose the name Gregory.

A couple of weeks later, Garrett announced that he wanted to write his life story. I thought it was a great idea, and we decided that he would talk and I would write. His first words were those that still remain at the front of his book: "This is the true story of Garrett Porter and my trials and triumphs."

Writing his book was a marvelous experience for him and for me as well. We laughed and we cried, and we relived everything—every trial and triumph—again.

As time went on, I became more and more aware that Garrett was not just writing the book for fun or for therapy. From the beginning, he was visualizing it being published. We put his book and my article as an appendix together, and I sent it to John White who, after reading it, agreed to be our literary agent.

From the beginning, this book generated a lot of interest, and a number of publishers asked John to see it and wrote warm and complimentary letters back with their rejections. It seemed that everyone recognized the power and beauty of Garrett's book, but they all thought it was too short to publish. And when we and Caroline Myss and Stillpoint found each other, they still thought it was too short. However, they asked me to write a book around a book, positioning Garrett's story within the context of my work, in general, and within a context of what makes for psychophysiologic self-regulation and healing.

In writing this book, we have several audiences in mind. Garrett wrote his book, as he makes eminently clear, to show that, far from being a miracle, he worked very hard to achieve what he did, and anyone can do it. Anyone can do it because that's all it is—no miracle, just work.

As I have been writing this, I have been very aware of the rift that sometimes exists between traditional medicine and psychological practices that evoke the capacity for responsibility and participation of the patient. I have had physicians ask if it was not wrong, cruel, and unethical to suggest to patients that they might be able to alter the course of their own illness with visualization. If they were not succeeding, would they not feel more guilt and pain?

This question raises compassion in me, for I think it points out how terribly responsible physicians must feel when treatment fails.

But there can be no failure in trying. Everyone can be a success at trying, and trying brings strength and energy of its own, which is a healing force. When my mother was a little girl, she had tried hard to accomplish something which did not succeed, and one of her sisters told her, "You did your best, and even the angels can't do better than that." I have shared this story with my patients—and others—many times.

None of us can postpone death forever, and a cure does not confer immortality on anyone, and yet this often seems to be the unconscious agenda of both physician and patient. Perhaps this is at the root of the great fear of conveying false hope to a patient. Even many of my colleagues who work with visualization and imagery are wary of giving false hope. How could HOPE ever be false? In this life there are never any guarantees, and this is especially true for people facing catastrophic and life-threatening illness. But there is always hope for something. Hope for a better day, for more comfort, for some joy and fun. Hope for less pain. Even hope for a more aware, more comfortable death, closure with loved ones accomplished.

The point is, hope has a neuroendocrinological effect on the body—hope affects brain chemistry, beliefs have biological consequences. One thing is absolutely certain—none of us will get out of here alive. "You can't take it with you" is surely true of our bodies. In the meantime, isn't it better to end life fully engaged in the effort to be well, to enjoy each day to the fullest, to strive for what we wish for rather than to contract, give up, and turn inward in helplessness and despair?

We give lip service to the importance of quality of life but then seem to forget it in much of our practices. In a November issue of the *Journal of the American Medical Association*, in the Commentary, "Death is Not the Enemy," Landau and Gustafson wrote: "An intense preoccupation with the preservation of physical life, however, seems sometimes to be based on an assumption that death is unnatural, or that its delay, even briefly, through medical and technical means is always a triumph of human achievement over the limitations of nature. It is as if death is in every case an evil, a kind of demonic power . . ." This view of death makes wellness much harder to achieve.

Wise men and religious teachers throughout the ages have counseled aspirants to make friends with their death. Far from being the enemy, death is the last great adventure that this life has to offer. Dying is something that everyone ever born on this planet before us has done, that everyone now living will do, and that everyone yet to come will also do. A recognition of the impermanence of the physical body makes each moment more precious; living more fully in the "here and now" makes death more easy to accept.

Patients can learn to encounter death in a conscious, intentional manner and participate more fully in their death just as they can learn to participate more fully in healing and in living consciously. Very early in working with patients, I tell them that the work that we are about to do together is a healing process, and it can be a healing for wellness or for a more healing death. Every patient needs to know that death is not the enemy, that it is something that all humans share, and that they can learn to use self-regulation and visualization to promote pain control and peace of mind if and when they are moving toward death. Elisabeth Kübler-Ross, who worked with hundreds of dying cancer patients, now says that she would prefer cancer as a means of death if given the opportunity to choose, because it provides time for closure, for finishing unfinished business, saying goodbye to loved ones, and because it allows for the possibility of maintaining continuity of consciousness during the dying process.

All of the patients I worked with who have died felt that the process of learning self-regulation and a different self-concept were rewarding and worthwhile. It is not uncommon for patients confronting catastrophic illness to remark that it is the best time of their lives, even though they are sick. And families of patients frequently affirm this also and feel that what was accomplished in the way of self-awareness, self-mastery, and the accompanying changes of attitude made the rest of life, and death, not only more comfortable but also more meaningful.

Garrett was not alone among my patients to experience his "inner body." Approximately one-quarter of the persons I have worked with who were encountering catastrophic illness have had out-of-body experiences, most frequently connected with surgery. Invariably such experiences alleviate the fear of death. They feel that they have had a profound and meaningful encounter with death and lived through it, and they know that they will "live" through it again.

The experience almost always includes seeing one's own body from a distance and being aware of still having a "body" of a different nature. It may also include being met by friends and relatives who have died, or being confronted by a "being of light," or seeing one's life in a panoramic overview, often with a dispassionate and compassionate understanding of the deeper meaning of the events of that life. Always these experiences are accompanied by feelings of *love, joy,* and *peace.* Quite frequently, these people feel a purpose and meaning to their lives that they had not felt before. Experiences such as these have been written of extensively by Stanislav Grof and Joan Halifax, Kenneth Ring, Raymond Moody, and Glen Gabbard and Stuart Twemlow.

By waking up to the possibilities of change and transformation, we can re-choose, reconceptualize, and respond differently. Those who engage in this task gain an understanding of the phenomenal power of the mind and of our natural inner ability to heal ourselves. Our self-image and our beliefs can either imprison us, set limitations on our capacities, or they can liberate us, help us heal and be whole.

It seems to me that what can emerge from all the new areas of research can be a wholistic approach in the very best sense of the word. A combination of the very best that medical science has to offer, including the new findings in oncogenes, the body's ability to repair damaged DNA in lymphocytes, receptor sites for neurotransmitters on lymphocytes, monoclonal antibodies, and more and more refined chemotherapeutic agents; from psychoneuroimmunology and the burgeoning research into all the mind-behavior-body mechanisms; and from the most important resource of all, the individual's own internal resources for being a full partner in every aspect of his/her treatment, can create a wonderful synergy to optimize healing and wellness, can create a true science of health.

An adventure in consciousness is worthwhile whether the adventure is for a day, a week, a year or a decade. Actually in every task of life the joy is in the doing—the activity is its own reward—and once the task is accomplished there is that momentary glow of satisfaction, and then we need to get on with it. On to the next task, the next effort, on with BEING and BECOMING.

Perhaps dying is like that too—a momentary glow of accomplishment, and then getting on with it again.

The work we do with cancer patients is often called adjunctive cancer therapy. Adjunctive means in addition to and in support of; and the psychological and psychophysiological work is in addition to and in support of, medical treatment. The two are synergistic, and both have an important—an essential—contribution to make to the well-being of the patient.

Garrett and I would like this to be a book that physicians will feel glad to give to their patients—a guideline to an extra ingredient of wellness, and an inspiration for an extra measure of participation and hope.

ACKNOWLEDGMENTS

I want to thank Garrett Porter, my co-author and first cancer patient. His courage, wisdom, and persistence were an inspiration and contributed greatly to my knowledge and confidence in working with other patients. I also want to thank all my patients and friends, named and unnamed, whose willingness to take responsibility for self-regulation and to participate in a healing process have made this work possible.

The Menninger Foundation has provided a wonderful place to work and grow as well as the freedom and stimulation to develop new ideas and new ways of working on the relationships of mind and body. I wish to thank particularly Dr. Roy Menninger, the president of the Foundation, for setting an atmosphere that supports an open-minded quest for knowledge; and Dr. Karl Menninger who has been a guiding light in my thinking about imprisonment and liberation, from his views of penal justice in "The Crime of Punishment" to his understandings of the human struggle for self-actualization and self-regulation.

I want to thank the entire staff of the Voluntary Controls Program for their friendship, support, and contributions to my growth. Dr. Elmer and Alyce Green initiated a conceptual framework restoring human potential to its rightful place in the healing arts, and they then provided a climate where my colleagues and I could put these concepts into practice.

Thanks, and the greatest appreciation and respect, are due to my friends and colleagues and the many researchers and clinicians working at the leading edge of the study of mind and immunity. In particular, Dr. Steven Locke, Dr. Paul Rosch, Dr. Gerald Jampolsky, Stephanie Matthews-Simonton and Dr. Carl Simonton have been personally helpful to me. Warm thanks and appreciation go to Milton Friedman, who gave freely of his writing skills and his wisdom in making many valuable suggestions during the preparation of this manuscript.

I also wish to express appreciation to the Biofeedback Society of America and the many colleagues who are providing inspiration and guidelines in the emerging field of self-regulation therapies. These pioneering efforts have helped to bring about a paradigm shift in which empowerment for healing and voluntary control is vested primarily in the individual's own self rather than in external agents.

Most of all, I want to express deepest appreciation to my husband, colleague, and best friend, Dr. Steven Fahrion, whose input and support all the way from formatting my disks to typing the bibliography has made this work easier and more fun.

*. . . For in every action what is primarily
intended by the doer, whether he acts from
natural necessity or out of free will, is the
disclosure of his own image . . . Thus,
nothing acts unless by acting it makes
patent its latent self.*

—DANTE

*Recent conceptual developments in the
mind-brain sciences rejecting reductionism
and materialistic determinism on the one
side, and dualisms on the other, clear the
way for a rational approach to the theory
and prescription of values and to a natural
fusion of science and religion.*

—ROGER SPERRY

CHAPTER ONE

The Therapist's Story

When I first saw Garrett, he was sitting in a reclining chair, hooked up to a machine with flashing red lights and a humming sound. His straight brown hair fell almost to his eyebrows, and clear shining eyes peered out beneath. He was nine years old and not tall for his age, but somehow his presence was so solid, so compelling, that I never really thought of him as small. Looking back, I realize we never really had the relationship of an adult and a child. In the most natural and unpretentious way, Garrett always thought of himself, and acted as, an equal partner. We embarked on an adventure together, teaching and learning as we went along.

I was being consulted to work with Garrett on visualization and imagery, to help him mobilize all his body's resources, and especially his immune system, in a crucial battle. In September 1978, less than two months earlier,

Garrett had been diagnosed as having an inoperable brain tumor.

Garrett was hooked up to a biofeedback machine. With its help, and under the able guidance of my husband and colleague, Dr. Steven Fahrion, he had been learning to control with his mind some of the things his body was doing. He had learned that by imagining that his hands were warm, he could make them very warm at will, and by visualizing himself as limp and relaxed, he could make his muscles almost completely quiet. He was quite good at it and was already beginning to get a sense of how his mind affected and controlled his body.

Garrett was receiving radiation treatment. His mother and father, Sue and Richard Porter, wanted to do everything they could to aid the healing process. Garrett's grandmother had died of cancer earlier in the year. In the process of helping her, they had obtained one of the Simonton tapes. Dr. Carl Simonton and Stephanie Simonton pioneered the recent work using imagery and visualization to unleash the powers of the mind and the immune system.

Garrett had been using the Simonton tape, but in our first meeting he informed me that he thought the tape was too boring for kids. He wanted us to make a tape that kids would like. Making this tape became our first task together.

Before I continue with the story of my work with Garrett, I think it is appropriate that I, like Garrett, address the question of "Why Me?" Why does someone choose the healing profession? Most of this book is about human potential, about our natural capacity to grow, to heal, to create change, our ability to influence everything that happens inside us. This is a relatively new idea in Western thinking. But it was not a new idea to me at the time I met Garrett.

Childhood Memories
Early Preparation and Training

From childhood I had been immersed in ideas and concepts from the East as well as from the West. I had the opportunity to grow up in a family that, as far back as the World War II era, explored and studied ideas that are just now emerging into Western consciousness, just now gaining the attention and the gradual acceptance of the scientific community. My parents, Elmer and Alyce Green, were integrating studies of physics and metaphysics from both Eastern and Western scientific and philosophical perspectives. Elmer was a physicist during my childhood, high school, and college years, and the influences on my life and thought from science and metaphysics were experiential as well as cognitive. The concepts that influenced my childhood had much to do with self-regulation and mind-body unity.

In the 1920's, the mainstream of psychology had turned its back on the "psyche" as the proper subject of study. Psychology abandoned such concepts as awareness, will, and consciousness in order to meet its increasingly narrow view of what was considered "scientific." But my family's assumptions were more along the lines of the thinking of William James who wrote, "The divorce between scientific facts and religious facts may not necessarily be as eternal as it first seems . . . The rigorously impersonal view of science may one day appear as having been a useful eccentricity rather than the definitely triumphant position which the sectarian scientist at present so confidently announces it to be."

Shortly after William James' great contributions to psychology, which are once again capturing the interest and imagination of many psychologists, mainstream psychology turned sharply away from possible associations with religion and philosophy and turned so much toward the "rigorously impersonal" that it led one psychologist to joke that, "First psychology lost its soul, then it lost its mind, and finally it lost consciousness."

In my own study of psychology in college, I was excruciatingly aware that the psychology I was learning did not fit my experience. I *knew* from my own internal experience that body follows mind, that we operate on the basis of our mental self-image and self-concept, that imagery initiates action. In other words, I anticipated that the subject matter of psychology would be consciousness.

For reasons of fitting in and winning approval as well as for the reason of grades, I *had* to be, and I wanted to be, mainstream in what I espoused. I remember my delight on discovering the concept of *logic tight compartments* with great glee, and I became fond of saying, "The apparent differences between science and religion lie in our ignorance." I still firmly believe this. There is much we don't know about how the world works, who and what we are, the nature of mind, the nature of life, the nature of reality— but whatever the "truth" is, I feel certain that it will be internally consistent.

Consciousness was a major factor in my awareness as I was growing up. Remonstrations often took the form of "Be Conscious" and "Be Aware." "Don't be unconscious" was a familiar phrase. The interests of my parents in Eastern as well as Western thought also brought me into association with individuals with highly-developed capacity for self-regulation. Their unusual abilities were simply taken for granted among us children, as children will take for granted everything which occurs within their realm of experience. Yogic capacities for self-regulation were part of my experience. The role the mind can play in healing was an ordinary, if not always experienced, fact.

The relationship between mind and body was always explicit in my family as I was growing up. I remember phrases from my early childhood like, "You are the boss of your stomach," if my tummy hurt, or, "See if you can make the feeling disappear or turn into a different kind of feeling with your mind," if I complained of itching from a mosquito bite.

When I was eleven, we lived in Canada for a brief period in the wintertime. We occupied a house that was constructed to be a summer house on the shore of Victoria Bay. It had a big porch from which one could throw stones to the water's edge at high tide. There was a fireplace in the living room and a big wood-burning stove for heating and cooking in the kitchen. Other than these two comforts, there was no heat.

There were a number of large bedrooms upstairs in the house, and my brother Doug and I each had one. Our younger sisters slept downstairs where it was warmer, as did our parents. It was so cold upstairs that each morning when I woke up, the water in the bowl on my dresser was frozen. Grabbing my clothes, I would hurry downstairs and dress in the kitchen next to the glowing woodstove which was warming the whole room. At night the process was reversed, and going upstairs was delayed until the last minute when, pajama clad, I would rush upstairs and leap between icy sheets. There, curled into a tight ball, I would shiver.

After a few nights of this, my Dad came into the room

one evening and saw my misery. "Just stretch out your legs and send the blood down into your feet—imagine that you are holding your feet out towards the stove and your feet are becoming warmer and warmer," he told me. This worked almost immediately, and soon my feet and legs were snug and warm under the blankets. This technique kept me warm in Canada, and it has helped me many times since, on camping trips, playing in the snow, and skiing. At that time, there were no biofeedback instruments, but I had my own sensory biofeedback as I felt my feet become tingly and radiant.

So the fact of self-regulation was not new to me. In some ways it was a natural skill, as natural an event as being able to walk or speak. An expectation that I could learn to quiet my stomach ache or heal a sore throat did not seem different in any way from the expectation that I could learn to play tennis or drive a car.

And as will be seen, the expectation for self-healing became just as natural for Garrett as he learned from experience that his mind could control his body.

With the advent of sensitive instruments that can provide information about body processes in which we *don't* get much sensory feedback, such as information about what our hearts are doing or how much acid our stomachs are secreting, it is becoming clear to all who practice physiologic self-regulation (and gradually proven to the scientific community too) that with our minds and our self-created images (visualizations) we can change our heartbeat or our stomach acid by intention.

This sure knowledge—the experiential awareness of self-regulation—was laid aside, or at least not integrated into my "other" learning, as I studied academic and clinical psychology. Most of my early professional career was largely diagnostic work. First I was an assistant to the Court Psychologist in Santa Barbara, California, and then I was a psychologist at the New York Guild for the Jewish Blind and later at the Brooklyn Psychiatric Centers. I was also learning individual and group psychotherapy under professional supervision and enjoying it very much, yet it was still separate philosophically and strategically from my inner sense of human potential.

The Menninger Foundation: Voluntary Controls Program

In the spring of 1970, I left New York and came to Topeka, Kansas, for what I thought would be a visit, albeit a long one, with my family. It was an exciting and enriching time in the Voluntary Controls Program at The Menninger Foundation, and I soon had an opportunity to be a part of it.

Elmer and Alyce Green had decided both to pursue their interest in self-regulation and volition and to develop ways to teach people to become conscious of, and to learn voluntary control of, physiological and psychological processes that are ordinarily unconscious. This led them first to the University of Chicago for graduate education in Psychology and then to The Menninger Foundation where they soon established the Voluntary Controls program. This coincided with the twelve years I spent in New York. By the time I came to visit them in Topeka, they had already completed much of the groundwork for what they intended to accomplish in making self-regulation objective, measurable, and verifiable.

Elmer and Alyce had been instrumental in helping to

organize the founding meeting of the Biofeedback Research Society in 1969, and soon this new scientific endeavor began to attract national attention. This helped to bring them an opportunity to examine the self-regulatory skills of a few "unusual" individuals who were brought to their attention.

The first of these was Swami Rama, an accomplished Yogi from Rishikesh, India. One day Elmer received a phone call from Dr. Daniel Ferguson, a psychiatrist who had graduated from the Menninger School of Psychiatry, and was practicing in St. Paul, Minnesota. Dr. Ferguson asked if Elmer would be interested in examining, under laboratory conditions, a yogi with unusual psychophysiologic control. The possibilities were intriguing.

Swami Rama came for a visit in the Spring of 1970. Arrangements were then made for him to return for an extended period in the fall. At the same time, Elmer and Alyce were planning a pilot project on theta brain wave training for imagery and creativity. I had the opportunity to take part as one of the research subjects. This was an opportunity I couldn't pass up, although it meant a commitment of approximately a year to complete the research.

In order to remain in Topeka for that length of time, I had to find a job, and before long I was employed as a clinical psychologist at the Kansas Reception and Diagnostic Center. This intake center evaluated prisoners who had been convicted of a crime and sentenced. The Center sought to determine whether they should be sent on to another institution to serve sentence or to receive probation.

My clinical experience as a psychologist had given me little preparation for what I would find "behind the walls." I knew nothing about the penal system or the justice system and like most people, had entertained many misconceptions. It took me some time to even *see* who these inmates were, as my perceptions were so clouded by my preconceived notions.

I was expecting to find hardened, exploitive men who deliberately chose to live a life of crime to get something for nothing by preying on society. I was surprised by their youth and even more surprised by the sense of helplessness that most of them conveyed. I began to see that most of them held very negative self-images, and this fact was a major determinant of much of their behavior.

The Diagnostic Center afforded the opportunity of working with groups, and eventually I developed a program that became a research project. In designing the project, I wanted to accomplish two things: first, to create a learning experience for prisoners that would parallel and incorporate ideas from my own learning experiences; and second, to provide the men who would be serving time in prison with some conceptual framework and coping techniques which could help make their prison experience less devastating.

The mind operates according to its image of itself, and the self-image we hold is like a blueprint for our behavior and it shapes our experiences. This is a major premise. Our behavior is controlled by the visualizations we hold, consciously or unconsciously. *If we wish to change some aspect of our life, we must first become aware of the images we hold and then create visualizations for the changes we wish to see come into being.*

Thus it seemed clear that to help inmates find a way to change their experience, their perceptions, and their behavior, it would be necessary to give them new insights into who they were, to help them gain a positive self-image. Increased self esteem could help them engage the world in a more positive manner. This was my first opportunity to put into practice a conceptual model for transformation based on growth, optimal functioning, and self-actualization.

This consciousness training program for prisoners evolved from the convergence of the three major areas of learning and growth that were going on in my life at the time. One was the experience of working and being in a prison setting, with all that this entailed; another was the work and teaching I was doing with guided imagery and Psychosynthesis; and the third was my experience with biofeedback as a theta subject in the brain wave training biofeedback research project. These were at first separate learning areas which gradually began to merge.

The Progoff Method

While I was still living in New York City, I met Dr. Ira Progoff and began working with his Intensive Journal method of inner dialogue. Dr. Progoff, a noted depth psychologist and a student and interpreter of Dr. Carl Jung, had developed this unique and powerful method of teaching perception of inner reality and unconscious processes.

The Progoff method is instrumental in establishing a bridge by which a person's outer life and inner experience can be linked in a meaningful way. Techniques which provide deep insight into the "raw materials" of the inner self and integrate them for use in the outer world are systematically taught, using a psychological workbook method called The Intensive Journal.

Participants in Dr. Progoff's group and individual therapy learn to use their acquired techniques for creative problem-solving and continued growth in their daily lives. I read a number of his books and took several workshops on personal self-exploration.

Psychosynthesis: Merging Psychology, Philosophy and Intuition

Progoff's training methods are similar and complementary to the psychological method of Psychosynthesis. Psychosynthesis is a psychological/educational approach to therapy which is concerned with the development of the whole person. It views each individual as a whole and accords to every level of being—physical, emotional, mental, and spiritual—its due importance. A basic tenet in psychosynthesis is the existence of a central Self, viewed, as in Jungian psychology, as an active center within a person through which integration—synthesis—takes place. Its founder, Robert Assagioli, M.D., was a colleague of Freud and Jung who in 1910 pioneered in bringing psychoanalysis to Italy. Assagioli felt that psychoanalysis contributed to an understanding of human nature and to one's self-understanding. He believed, however, that to understand antecedents of present problems was insufficient for psychological healing. He devised guidelines for integrating insights and for conscious self-creation and growth.

Assagioli had himself created a much larger synthesis. During the time he was studying the emerging psychoanalytic theory, he was also a student of a Tibetan teacher whose philosophy encouraged self-regulation and taking responsibility consciously for one's personal and spiritual growth. Recognizing that psychoanalysis left out the higher aspects of human nature and generally limited itself to digging in the "basement of the human psyche" (Freud's own description), Assagioli evolved a more comprehensive theoretical framework. This framework follows a developmental line from Freud through Jung and later Abraham Maslow, and employs an eclectic approach to facilitating personal growth.

I first became acquainted with psychosynthesis when I read the book of that title by Assagioli. More than any other "school" of psychology, psychosynthesis felt familiar and right to me. It fit my world view, philosophical premises, and conceptual framework about the nature of man. When I read the book, I was delighted to see some of these concepts expressed as psychological theory with practical guidelines for therapeutic applications and personal exploration. Discovering psychosynthesis brought together my philosophical beliefs and my professional psychotherapeutic knowledge, welding them into an integrated and unified whole.

When I came to Kansas I pursued psychosynthesis in a number of workshops. Later I visited the Psychosynthesis Institute in California and spent time consulting with James and Susan Vargiu, its directors. They gave me ideas and guidelines in my plans to set up a pilot psychosynthesis group in Topeka with professional colleagues. I formed a small group of people interested in exploring psychosynthesis as a therapeutic technique.

The group included two psychiatrists and their wives, a psychiatric nurse, a social worker, a rehabilitation counselor, and two other psychologists besides myself. We met for a year. The group studied Dr. Assagioli's writings, discussed the concepts and techniques, applied many of the techniques in group sessions, and also did intensive self-exploration with guided imagery in a number of ways. We discussed what we were doing and compared it to other psychological methods and theory.

The next year, I formed a class through a local organization that operated like a growth center, sponsoring lectures and classes. There were about forty people enrolled in this class which also lasted for almost one year, meeting weekly. The exercises, techniques which I developed, and group experiences formed the basis for the group work I later conducted in the prison system.

The Simontons' Pioneer Work in Visualization Therapy

The first time I heard of Carl and Stephanie Simonton, or thought much about cancer, occurred during this class. One of the members brought a newspaper clipping describing the Simontons' work with cancer patients at Travis Air Force Base in California. The article told how Dr. Simonton gave the patient the clearest possible image of their actual physical condition at the time, as well as a clear mental picture of the ideal outcome of radiation treatment to the cancer site. The patients were then instructed to visualize during their radiation treatments, as well as several other times each day, their body moving toward and achieving that ideal picture of perfect healing. It was a unique application of psychosynthesis in action to promote physical healing.

Biofeedback and Imagery: Keys to Visualization Training

For my group work with prisoners, I was planning a "consciousness training program" and exploration into self, using primarily psychosynthesis and guided imagery. I had some reservations about the willingness and readiness of this group to engage in imagery, introspection, and self-exploration. The concept of imagery was a turn-off to many of them. The very word "imagination" denoted pretense or phoniness as in the sentence, "It's only your imagination." In general, they were coming from a context of "be practical, be realistic, don't daydream." They were action-oriented and externally-oriented. These are generalizations, and there were notable exceptions, but largely I was working with a group for whom meditation, introspection, and just being quiet with one's self was a rare or nonexistent experience.

The solution to this problem emerged from experiences with biofeedback. I decided to incorporate biofeedback training into the program. Successful biofeedback training also uses imagery. The images may be more or less elaborated, but however simple or elaborate, some kind of image always precedes the action. A person who is warming his hands may visualize himself lying on a beach in the warm sun with the sun shining down on him, making his hands warmer and warmer. Another person might use a more mechanical image of the blood flowing down through the vasculature of their arms and into their hands. Even more simply, a person might hold an image of warm hands.

There must be some sort of image of what is desired or intended in order for any voluntary change to occur. In other words, the visualization or representation of the act is a necessary prerequisite to voluntary action.

The use of imagery in psychotherapy is as old as the history of psychotherapy itself; it was first reported in modern western psychotherapy in the famous case of Anna O. by Breuer and Freud in 1895 in their publication, *Studies In Hysteria.*

Freud recognized the primacy and potency of imagery.

It is possible for thought processes to become conscious through a reversion to visual residues and in many people this seems to be a favorite method. Thinking in pictures ... approximates more closely the unconscious processes than does thinking in words, and it is unquestionably older than the latter, both ontogenetically and phylogenetically.[1]

The use of imagery has a long and fascinating history and is currently enjoying widespread application.

Everything fell into place with this recognition: imagery is the link. It was primarily self-image upon which I wanted to have an effect with my consciousness training program. Imagery initiates all conscious physical activity, from reaching for an object, to skiing, playing tennis, and placing a golf ball on the green. Imagery precedes thought phylogenetically and developmentally, and I believe (and considerable evidence is accumulating for the thesis) that imagery initiates all thought processes, associations, and all secondary-process thinking.

A primary tenet of psychosynthesis is that *imagery precedes action.* Now, in the work with visualization and healing, it becomes obvious that imagery precedes physiological action within the body as well as action in the world.

Victim Consciousness: A Debilitating Mythology

Strange as it may seem, the work that I did with the prisoners proved very influential in developing some of the deepest concepts of visualization and imagery work with patients. This is especially true for people who have cancer and other life-threatening illnesses. There is a tendency on the part of both prisoners and patients to think of themselves as victims; there is also a tendency on the part of society to think of both groups as victims.

The prisoners I worked with thought of themselves (and were thought of by others) as victims of society, of cultural deprivation, poor education, lack of opportunity, poverty, broken homes, alcoholic parents, abusive parents, chaotic instability, or extreme external stress from a wide variety of causes. Even more important, they were victims of their own defenses, of their identifications, of self-defeating and self-destructive behavior, of tension and anxiety and low frustration tolerance and poor impulse control, and of internal, physiological and psychological stress.

People who have cancer are often referred to as cancer *victims*. They think of themselves, and are thought of by society, as victims of external physical causes such as carcinogens in our air and our food, and of psychosocial stress such as loss and bereavement. Perceiving oneself as a victim can make one feel like a passive recipient of life events rather than an active participant.

Victim consciousness engenders feelings of helplessness and hopelessness that can contribute to the progress of disease. An important, perhaps an essential, component of healing is a feeling of empowerment, of self-mastery, physiologically and psychologically.

Taking Responsibility for Disease

In order for healing to take place from the inside, there must be a feeling of *responsibility*. There must be a sense that mind and body are *connected*, that our bodies and our health have a capacity for responsiveness. We must believe in and experience a capacity for self-regulation, a knowledge that volition can have an impact on outcome.

At the same time, it is crucial to realize that responsibility does not mean, or imply, guilt. One of the objections frequently heard against taking responsibility through the use of visualization and imagery as an aid in cancer treatment is the contention that it makes people feel guilty for having cancer, that it should never be suggested that they are responsible for their condition.

This is one of the most difficult subjects to tackle and also one of the most important. Most emerging literature concerned with the genesis of cancer points out the relationships between stress and cancer, between loss or bereavement and the onset of malignancies. Although the existence of a "cancer personality" is still controversial, most researchers report pre-existing depression and see repression and denial as frequent defense mechanisms. If all of the body's resources are to be brought to bear in a healing process, these internal attitudes need to be changed.

All of us are products of our past learning and experiences, and our attitudes and behavior are reflections of, and to a large extent determined by, this past. We learn and experience many things before we have any ability to control them. In fact, most educators and psychologists agree that our major behavior patterns and coping styles are learned during the first five to seven years of life. So, in this one very real sense, we are not responsible for what we believe, feel, and do, for what we are, or what we have become. But as long as we stay locked in a belief system which includes a victim consciousness, our capacity for true volition is curtailed, and we do not express personal, self-directed power.

It is not easy to accept responsibility for future events without feeling guilty for past events. Nevertheless, in the presence of proper motivation, insight, or environment, or a combination of these, *we can at any moment accept what we presently are and begin to assume responsibility for what we are becoming.* It depends in part on our awareness of "becoming." All insight therapy and expressive therapy depend on our human capacity to assume a measure of responsibility for the direction of our lives by helping us change what we believe, feel, and do.

Garrett

Garrett knew this very well. He understood intuitively about what it means to take responsibility for oneself. At a time when he was the most depressed, when he fell and was unable to get up, when he felt as though death was imminent, he came to realize that he could take responsibility. He wondered:

> *"Is this happening to me? It is too fast, and I am not supposed to die. I'm only nine years old and it is not fair"... We were about ready to go out and buy the coffin. I mean, I was at the bottom. I was at death's door. I kept going to school and kept trying to stay active, but I would just get lower and lower. It was a pain in the butt to go to school and a pain in the butt to do anything. I wasn't in physical pain, but I was so depressed. I didn't realize what depression was; I just got down there.*
>
> *One night I was lying in bed thinking and looking at myself in an overall view of things and I said, "My*

*God, Garrett this is what you are." Suddenly it hit
me; there has got to be something I can do. It just
came to me. It just dawned ... a voice came out and
said, "Garrett, you have to make a choice. You can
either go ahead and go the way you are and
die—AND DIE—or you can fight and possibly win
... POSSIBLY." I wasn't sure. It was a chance ... It
was just like a light shining on me.*

Garrett discovered that he could make a choice to put
his effort in living. In my office the next time, he stated
clearly and strongly "I choose to *live*," even though, as he
explained, he recognized it as a *possibility*, as something to
work for day by day. That adventure—in and of itself—
became a purpose for living.

The same principle was described by Norman Cousins
in talking about choices he made ("What I Learned From
3000 Doctors"). When he was diagnosed with cardiovascu-
lar disease, he noticed his reaction was like looking down
two roads; he could choose between limiting his activities
or increasing his exercise. He chose the second road because it "might carry me for a few months or a few weeks
or a few minutes, but it was *my road.*"

Accepting responsibility is a cause for joy and optimism. A number of patients have expressed great relief
upon the realization that there *is* something that they can
do for themselves, that they can participate in a healing
venture, and that they need not feel there is nothing they
can do to help themselves.

The question of guilt cannot be ignored altogether,
however, and has to be resolved. I have had patients who
felt guilty because they smoked and had lung cancer. I
have had patients who felt guilty because they considered

that they had abused their bodies; and I have had patients who felt guilty because they were or were not receiving specific treatments.

One woman, for whom chemotherapy was not recommended, constantly felt some guilt that she was not receiving chemotherapy, since one physician, who favored it, told her that there might be "a mother cancer lurking in there somewhere."

This topic will be discussed more fully in Chapter Six on attitudes, beliefs and expectations. For now, suffice it to say that in order to facilitate a climate for change, for healing and transformation, it is essential to dispense with guilt and blame and to concentrate one's attention and efforts on the here and now and on what can be done from hence forward.

Research on the Connection between Conscious and Unconscious Processes

One more event happened during my years at the Diagnostic Center that was of major significance to my work with cancer patients. I had an opportunity to take part in the LSD training program for professionals, a research program being conducted by Stanislov Grof, M.D., and colleagues at the Maryland Psychiatric Research Hospital in Spring Grove, Maryland. The program for professionals was one part of a large research project on the relevance of LSD to therapy, to self knowledge, and to forming a temporary wide-open access between conscious and unconscious processes.

My single experience with LSD was deeply moving and significant, but what I wish to mention here is that another area of LSD research was a program administering LSD to selected terminal cancer patients to help alleviate pain and fear and make the transition to death an easier one.

During the week I spent at Spring Grove preparing for, having, and debriefing from my own LSD experience, I had the opportunity to view a number of tapes of these sessions with cancer patients. A colleague of Stan Grof in this work was Loch Rush. I had known both Stan and Loch for a long time, and Loch was also on my Doctoral Committee, so I was permitted to spend a good deal of time "behind the scenes," so to speak.

Witnessing these tapes had a powerful impact on me. In the book, *The Human Encounter with Death*, by Stanislov Grof, M.D. and Joan Halifax, Ph.D., Stan says:

> *The changes that occur in cancer patients following psychedelic therapy are extremely varied, complex, and multidimensional. Some of them are of a familiar nature, such as the alleviation of depression, tension, anxiety, sleep disturbance, and psychological withdrawal. Others involve phenomena that are quite new in Western psychiatry and psychology; especially specific changes in basic life philosophy, spiritual orientation and the hierarchy of values ... The clinical impressions of the often dramatic effects of LSD psychotherapy on the emotional condition of cancer patients was supported by the results of the ratings. The most pronounced therapeutic changes were observed in the areas of depression, anxiety, and pain, closely followed by those related to fear of death. The results were least dramatic in the area of medical management.*

I saw patients who were frightened, isolated and withdrawn, and in pain, emerging from their experience looking transformed. And they frequently acted transformed. They reduced their pain medication, took an interest in life, often began to paint or read or listen to music again, reassured their families and showed not only strength, but peace and even contentment. Seeing the dramatic and beautiful impact of experiential change of self-image, I decided at that point, in August of 1972, that I would some day like to do therapy with cancer patients. And although I thought of it often, it was to be more than six years before I would meet Garrett.

... the fact is that the approach to the numinous is the real therapy, and inasmuch as you attain to the numinous experience you are released from the curse of pathology. Even the very disease takes on a numinous character.

—CARL JUNG

To soar like an eagle, to see the world as a whole, to know the beauty that is wholeness, is to be sacred.

—DAVID CHETHLAHE PALADIN

CHAPTER TWO

Garrett Porter:
Portrait of A Hero

*W*hen Garrett was nine years old and just starting fourth grade, the presence of a right-hemisphere brain tumor, diagnosed as an astrocytoma, was confirmed by CAT scan. One morning in the late summer of 1978, he had awakened with his left arm feeling numb. At first, he and his parents thought perhaps he had slept on his arm, and indeed the numbness improved during the day. But a few days later, Garrett woke up with his arm completely paralyzed.

He was hospitalized for tests, and the diagnosis was made. The tumor was considered to be inoperable, and a course of radiation was recommended.

When Garrett's grandmother died of cancer earlier in the year, she was the third person in the family to die of cancer within eighteen months. Garrett's parents, Richard and Sue, are both professional health care workers. Richard is a social worker and Sue is a school counselor, and both have experience working with troubled patients and their families. When Richard's mother, grandmother, and aunt all died within eighteen months of each other, Richard and Sue began to look at the cancer literature. They concluded that there is a psychological component to cancer that needed to be confronted.

Before starting Garrett's treatment, his parents wanted to be certain that surgical removal of the tumor was not possible. They were told that the best place to go for an opinion about his tumor and information about his treatment was the Brain Tumor Research Institute of a University of California at San Francisco. They immediately went for a second opinion. The Brain Tumor Research Institute agreed with the diagnosis made in Topeka. The Institute also agreed that the tumor was inoperable, and radiation treatment was recommended.

When they returned to Topeka, radiation treatment was started at once. Richard and Sue also took Garrett to see Dr. Stephen Appelbaum, a friend and colleague, for a complete psychological workup. While at The Menninger Foundation, Steve Appelbaum was assigned to discover what could be learned from the new therapies. He described his investigations in his fascinating book *Out in Inner Space*. During the course of this work, he studied the Simontons' cancer therapy methods and eventually incorporated some of them into his psychological practice.

He concluded that Garrett was a very bright youngster with a lot of creative ability and said he would be interested in working with him. He gave Garrett the tape by Carl Simonton, "Relaxation and Mental Imagery for Cancer Therapy." Before the family returned Garrett became very sick, and so Steve Appelbaum referred the family to the Biofeedback and Psychophysiology Center.

Garrett's radiation treatment was nearing completion by Halloween. At this time Garrett was struggling with life and death decisions as well as a life-threatening illness. This was reflected in his choice of Halloween costume for that year, a mummy suit. His mother made it for him and he wore it seriously and with ironical humor. Even though this was a very difficult time for Garrett, he showed off his costume with a twinkle in his eye. This was only one of a myriad of ways that Garrett showed his ability to tackle problems symbolically.

Garrett was given what was considered to be the maximum medically-safe amount of radiation. Since chemotherapy would not be effective, and the tumor was inoperable, the family was told that everything medical that could be done *had* been done. His clinical symptoms continued to progress. They involved his left leg and, to some extent, the whole left side of his body.

Garrett's Therapy: All-out War on his Cancer

When Garrett and I decided to make a cassette tape of the visualization we would use to battle his tumor, it was Garrett's intention that we would make a tape that kids with tumors and cancer could use. He began his tape with, "You are about to experience a method used for fighting tumors and cancer."

There are two qualities that Garrett possesses that are very special and unusual: his sense of oneness with others and his deep inner sense of being of service to others. As I got to know Garrett, I came to realize that he understood intuitively John Donne's thought, ". . . No man is an is-

land unto himself, but each is a part of the main . . . Therefore, ask not for whom the bell tolls; it tolls for thee."

At that time, Garrett was a "Trekkie," in love with
Star Trek, Battlestar Galactica, and the whole idea of space
exploration. He organized the scenario for his visualization
around the idea of a space drama. He brought his electronic
game, "Battleship," to provide sound effects and make the
tape more realistic and exciting.

In Garrett's visualization, his programming ego (the
"self") is portrayed by Blue Leader, the leader of a squadron of fighter planes. His brain is represented by the solar
system, and his tumor is an invading planetoid which is
entering his solar system and threatening its existence. His
white cells and other immune defenses are represented by
the lasers and torpedoes with which the squadron of fighter
planes is armed.

My role was Ground Control, and by this device we
maintained a constant dialogue on the tape, creating the
visualizations as we went along. A complete transcription
of the tape is contained in Garrett's own story, "Why Me?"

In the taping, Garrett ran all the sound effects. He had
set the board up previously, with the battleships all con-
cealed. Each time he unleashed an attack against the planetoid, we really did not know whether it would be a hit or a
miss. This turned out to be fortuitous. This is how life really is; every day is not equally good, and every attack is
not equally effective. Garrett experienced good days and
not-so-good days, but from the beginning he seemed aware
that if he felt bad or did poorly one day, he could improve
the next.

If it were practical and safe to have daily CAT scans, I
am sure there would have been days in which the tumor
was growing and days in which the body's defenses were

reducing it, rather than a steady growth or decline as one might conceive when the process is taking place out of sight. I have often wondered, if we could have visually traced the entire history of the tumor, how much it would have reflected his clinical history in terms of ups and downs, and, especially, the turning point when he really started to improve.

In addition to this symbolic visualization, Garrett developed an organic, biological visualization. Eventually, he came to use the organic visualization most of the time. It was formed by taking an imaginary journey inside his brain on an exploration survey. As a tiny being, Garrett walked over the convolutions of his brain until he came to the tumor. His image of the tumor was that it looked like a chunk of raw hamburger, and in this image, as in his space battle, he described the tumor as looking "dumb." It is significant that in both the symbolic and the more organic visualizations, he saw the tumor as disorganized and somewhat powerless from the very beginning.

In his organic visualization, he saw hundreds, millions, of white cells attacking, chopping up, eating, and completely destroying the tumor. He drew several pictures of the white cells, portraying them as round balls with large mouths equipped with large, sharp teeth and eyes and a radar antenna that could seek out any enemy. As can be seen from Garrett's illustration, even though the cells are simple figures, they look effective and determined, somehow definite, but not vicious. From the beginning, he identified his white cells as competent and all-seeing.

Visualization and imagery formed the primary tools in Garrett's battle with his cancer. We also used guided imagery and unguided imagery for psychotherapy and for fun. These uses of imagery were part of a comprehensive program which included biofeedback-assisted self-regulation and deep relaxation. Attention was also given to basic health factors such as exercise and diet.

While all of this was going on, other psychological support systems were also brought into play. The family started working with a psychiatrist and friend at The Menninger Foundation, Dr. Joseph Hyland. Before long, Garrett himself opted out of these meetings, telling his parents, "You parents work with Dr. Hyland, I have my own people to work with." Dr. Hyland was seeing Garrett's parents regularly, and on occasion we all met together to discuss what was happening. On two occasions, meetings were arranged that included not only our teams but also his school teacher and principal. It is very important to have everyone involved who is participating, and it is especially helpful in dealing with trouble spots. Garrett's teacher that year had a very difficult time handling her feelings about a potentially dying child in the classroom, but the support of the other teachers, his fellow students and the principal, and the meetings we all held together, helped overcome what could otherwise have been an exceedingly negative school experience.

Garrett's illness changed the friendship system for the whole family. Some people became better friends, and other friends just disappeared, unable to face their own fears and discomfort over what to say or do. We all feel that the interpersonal relationships with those who remained friends were intensified and enhanced.

Garrett and I met on a weekly basis. In the beginning of the therapy, we spent quite a bit of time developing his self-regulation skills with the biofeedback equipment. He had learned to warm his hands from Steve Fahrion and was exceptionally good at it. I didn't learn until much later that this skill was especially important to him because he felt that this was one thing that he could do better than anyone else.

Garrett's perspective about learning to warm his hands was fascinating and informative. He said, "I went in there with an open mind. I was curious. I think that's what being a kid can do for you—because adults have this false sense of reality that maybe it's not possible. But I went in there with an open mind, and I thought it was really neat that I could control my body temperature. I made the connection that it was my mind that was really doing that."

Garrett also told me that when he took his temperature meter home to show to his parents, they were unable to warm their hands. This pleased Garrett. He explained, "Because I'd found something—you know, David's better at baseball and running and all those sports, and a lot of people are better at a lot of things than I am, and I hadn't really found something I was excellent at. Here was actually something I could do that no one else could do as well."

Because of the depth of his wisdom and intuition, his openness and self-insight, I could not really imagine that he might feel incompetent or inadequate. Nevertheless, learning these biofeedback skills in such an excellent way was really increasing his sense of competence and giving a big boost to his self-confidence.

Before long, Garrett could warm his hands to a maximum temperature as soon as he turned his attention to it. He could also turn his muscle tension down to very relaxed levels. These exercises were important not only in helping him to cope with the considerable stress he was under, but also in giving him *experiential* evidence of the capacity of his mental processes to direct his physiologic processes. A natural progression occurs from this, and it is more implicit than explicit: "I can send increased blood flow to my hand or my foot or my knee; I can relax my muscles to the point of turning off normal muscle tone; I can send my white cells to my tumor and increase my immune defenses all over my body."

For several months, Garrett's clinical symptoms continued to multiply. Eventually he had to wear a leg brace to help him to walk. He came to the point where if he fell down, it was impossible for him to get up unassisted. This was one of the most frightening and disheartening things that Garrett had to bear. But it also proved a prime motivation for his determination to fight for his life.

In February of 1979, another series of CAT scans were made of his brain, and these revealed that his tumor had grown considerably. His physicians concluded that no further medical treatment was indicated. As the radiotherapist later said, "We had shot our wad." At that time his prognosis was grim. It was believed that Garrett had less than a year to live.

Garrett's father said that the support of their physicians played a vital role in the well-being of the family. The doctors did more than people usually fantasize they do. Dr. Ralph Reymond, the radiotherapist, is both a physicist and a physician and was technically excellent. In addition to providing technical treatment, he also did a tremendous job of working with the family psychologically and socially. He said to Richard, "I tried to keep my distance, but Garrett wouldn't let me." He checked Garrett every day and was very accessible to the family. Garrett's parents feel they couldn't have survived as well as they did without their physicians, Dr. Reymond and Dr. Robert Parman, Garrett's pediatrician.

Honesty and Openness: Essential Ingredients

When the brain tumor was first diagnosed, Garrett had asked his father if it could kill him, and his father told him that it could. Later, Garrett revealed that he had wished at the time that his father had lied. I believe he already knew, unconsciously if not consciously, that the tumor could kill him, and that it would have been more upsetting if his father had deceived him.

There are at least two reasons why honesty and openness are essential. Falseness not only hinders communication, it also creates a barrier between conscious and unconscious knowledge. The aim in therapy is exactly the opposite: to create access to the unconscious, to bridge conscious and unconscious processes, and to increase conscious control of the unconscious.

It was important for Garrett to come to grips with whether he wanted to live. When Garrett wrote his own life story, he said that he was not sure that he wanted to go through the agony of it all. This was a serious question.

He was then seriously incapacitated, with little use of his left arm and difficulty in walking even in his leg brace, and for some time he was trapped if he fell down and no one was nearby to aid him. Garrett continued to go to school throughout the course of his treatment, and although it was very important for him to do so and to engage in a normal life as far as possible, he suffered some traumatic experiences. Once he fell down on the way to school and had to wait a very long time before someone came by to help. He was embarrassed and frightened.

Fighting The Disease Becomes a Way of Life

This was a frightening time for the whole family. A big change takes place in a family that is facing life-threatening illness. The future, once so sure, suddenly seems to disappear. For Richard Porter, reassurance came each evening when he came home from work and called Garrett from the bottom of the stairs. If Garrett answered, he knew he was still alive. For Sue, her reassurance was going in to wake him up each morning and seeing he was still alive.

Garrett told me, "I know my parents love me and want me to be safe and well, and that's why they tell me to be careful and walk better and stuff, but I don't want them to think about it so much—I don't want my life to be tumor, tumor, tumor all the time."

When this remark was shared with them, his parents were able to be incredibly responsive to it. Communication in the family became more and more open. Garrett's father subsequently remarked that it is very hard even for professionals to understand this sudden end of the future, when all the goals and dreams are suddenly questionable. But much good came from just living day to day. Each day became more precious, and life became enjoyable.

Until the brain tumor caused paralysis in his left arm, Garrett had been a "lefty." Now he had to develop new motor skills. Visual difficulties were also slowing his reading, and he was not doing as well in school as he wished or expected to do. Nevertheless, he carried on bravely with his activities as well as with his determination to live every day as a fight for life.

One of our goals in treatment was to help Garrett not only to *resolve* problems such as not being able to get up if he fell, but also to simultaneously *detoxify* them, "take some of the sting out." To help take the sting out of his problems with falling and getting up, we had a number of glorious pillow fights on the third floor of our clinic. In a large meeting room, there were stored enough gaily-patterned, large floor-type cushions to make a veritable castle mound in the middle of the floor. Steve often took part in these pillow fights, and occasionally other staff members could get in on the fun. The pillows were large enough so that if they were thrown right, we could knock others into the mound of pillows. Garrett was knocked down more than anybody. Sometimes we rolled him around on the pillows or buried him for good measure. We laughed so much our sides hurt, but more important than all the laughter and fun, Garrett began to learn techniques for struggling to his feet. He also began to like doing it.

Garrett's Dreams: A Source of Understanding

Early in his treatment process, when Garrett was having the most difficulty with questions of life and death, he had a number of experiences connected with dying. One day he told me that sometimes at night his "inner body" would come out of his body and float around in the living room, where he could see his mother and father. He was scared that he might be dying. He tried to get their attention, but he couldn't call out to them, "because I don't have my mouth with me." He felt as though he were drifting about uncontrollably, and his parents were getting farther and farther away. These experiences were both saddening and terrifying to him.

We found an entertaining way to cope with these fears in guided imagery connected with adventures in "out-of-body" experiences. The one he liked the best came from Cates' book, *The Awakened Mind.* This consisted of taking a trip on an airplane and becoming sleepy. While looking out of the window, half-asleep, he would think of how much fun it would be if he could fly. Suddenly, he would find himself sitting on the wing of the plane. Looking back in the window, he would see himself sitting in his seat on the plane, eyes closed and a smile upon his face. How terrific! He would fly round and round the plane, doing loop-the-loops, and then fly up to the front window and peer in. There would be the pilot and co-pilot, flying the plane and looking into the distance.

Garrett would wave and make faces at the crew, but of course they could not see him because he did not have his body with him. Then he would fly away from the plane, way, way up high until the plane looked like a tiny silver bug against the clouds. Then he swooped back down to sit on the wing again. After a bit, he would slide back into his body and wake up, thinking of the wonderful adventure and feeling of freedom in flying around without taking his body along. Garrett loved this type of imagery. Although it was only indirectly related to his more terrifying experiences, he ended up not being frightened by them, and they soon went away altogether.

Garrett Reaches to Give Meaning to his Therapy

One day when Garrett and I were talking and I wanted to refer to his *inner being,* or more permanent organizing self, I reminded him of what he had called his "inner body." He thought for a moment and then looked up with his intent gaze and said, "That's your *true self,* you know!"

During the early course of his illness, when his symptoms were most severe, I gave him Dr. Jerry Jampolsky's book, *There is a Rainbow Behind Every Dark Cloud.* This book was written by a group of children with catastrophic and life-threatening illnesses, primarily cancer, who were in a program for group support at the Center for Attitudinal Healing founded by Dr. Jampolsky. In this wonderful and inspiring book, the children share, in words and in pictures, their deepest fears and concerns, along with their joys, understandings, and coping techniques. The major elements include how they felt when they first learned they were sick; feelings about shots and radiation and losing hair; thoughts about death and dying; and choices they have to help themselves, including choosing peace instead of fear, and love instead of anger, and choosing to live "in the moment."

Garrett and I read this book together out loud. It was deeply meaningful to him, both a revelation and a relief. He kept saying "yeah, yeah" as different feelings were expressed. He actually got high on the book the first time we read it. It provided a wonderful release, and Garrett returned to it many times, especially in the beginning stages of our work together.

I also told Garrett about a newly-established telephone hotline for which Jerry Jampolsky had just received funding, which connected children from around the country who had life-threatening illnesses with children from the Center for Attitudinal Healing. The children could speak openly with each other since they knew that the person to whom they were talking knew what they were going through without any big explanation.

Garrett was very interested in joining the hotline. On the day I called the Center for Attitudinal Healing to add his name to the list, it happened (extraordinarily) that Jerry himself answered the phone. It also happened that at that minute a crew from CBS was at the Center making arrangements to film a segment for "60 Minutes" about the children and their work together. They wanted to include a sequence about the hotline and were in the process of looking for someone that the children could call for the filmed telephone conversation.

After talking to Garrett for a few minutes, Jerry asked him if he would like to receive that call. Garrett was delighted to be given the opportunity to take part in a national television show. A few months later, he was the voice on the "60 Minutes" show that said, "My name is Garrett, and I have a brain tumor."

The whole idea of the hotline was inspiring to Garrett; it captured his imagination. He soon decided that he would like to start a hotline of his own for children in Topeka. After considerable discussion and planning, Garrett's parents arranged his own special telephone line for hotline calls, with his own telephone number. A story appeared in the local newspaper telling about Garrett and the Center's hotline. It described Garrett's desire to start a hotline support system for local children with life-threatening illnesses, and his own special number was published.

We had anticipated that he might be inundated with calls. We also had some fantasies about calls from people in need other than those for whom the hotline was intended. Garrett had other telephone numbers to which he could refer callers, including such groups as "Can Help" and the Red Cross.

But at first Garrett's phone remained silent. Eventually, calls began coming in. His first contact was with an eighteen-year-old girl named Terri who had just been diagnosed as having a brain tumor. She was scared and despondent. When she called Garrett, they talked for more than an hour, and he told her all about himself, his treatment and feelings, and what he was doing to help himself with his own brain tumor. He also told her about the Center for Attitudinal Healing and its hotline. He felt it would be good for her to talk to someone her own age. I later learned that this conversation with Garrett was extremely important for her. It helped bring her out of a situational depression and did much to allay her fears and to give her a feeling of empowerment, a sense that there was something she could do to help herself.

Terri made several friends through the Center's hotline, but she and Garrett continued to talk. They became fast friends. They went on excursions together and later visited other children with cancer who had called Garrett on his hotline. The pair took one very ill youngster to the movies and the zoo, and they visited him in the hospital. This child did not live, yet Garrett and Terri had done much to make his last days more happy and fulfilled, less fearful and lonely.

Garrett still continued to get calls from the Center of Attitudinal Healing hotline, and soon a whole network of callers was established. His mother told me of one touching incident in which a young girl called who was frightened and upset and began to cry. Garrett shared his own similar fears and experiences. He then led her through some relaxation and visualization exercises right on the phone. They talked for a long time, and Garrett's mother commented that he seemed just like a professional therapist.

Actually, children can be the very best therapists for

each other. The Center for Attitudinal Healing acts on the belief that the two most powerful healing forces are choosing love instead of fear and being of service to others. It is very clear that choosing love and being of service were very important in Garrett's own self-healing process. Garrett was so calm and clear, with just the right combination of optimism and realism, and talking to him was of great benefit to a number of my patients, adults as well as children.

Garrett Turns the Corner: The Disease Weakens

As spring moved toward summer 1979, Garrett began to get better. Improvements included increased strength and use of his left arm and leg, learning to get up when he fell down, and in general, a greater appearance of health. He continued to do his visualizations every day, and I think he really enjoyed these experiences and never found them tedious.

Garrett came to the Biofeedback and Psychophysiology Center once a week to continue learning self-regulation and voluntary control as well as for visualization and imagery and play therapy. He made a lot of drawings, and most of the pictures he drew were concerned with the battles between various parts of his immune system and his tumor.

He began swimming, and he and I went swimming together in the Menninger pool as often as we could. His parents bought him some swim fins and a mask and snorkel, and he did well with these, swimming competently anywhere he wanted to go with confidence and joy.

When school resumed in the fall, Garrett returned with

renewed confidence, and he was able to perform better in his classes once again. His fifth grade teacher was supportive and also fostered his independence, helping him to maximize his strengths.

Victory: *The End of Planet Meatball!*

In late October, Garrett told me he had some exciting news. "I can't find my tumor in my imagery anymore," he said. "I think it's gone." He had never had any trouble visualizing the tumor before, and now, suddenly, it was entirely absent. He and I went on an exploratory tour of his brain, exploring all around. Everywhere he looked he saw only normal brain tissue.

The first time Garrett discovered his tumor to be absent was when he was doing his visualization at night before falling asleep. He was surprised to be unable to find it. He called his father and told him that the tumor was missing and that it must be gone. His Dad sat beside him and suggested that he try once more, and Garrett became very quiet and searched diligently. He then told his father that he could not find any tumor and that all he saw was a "funny white spot" where the tumor had been.

At the time, I received this news with mixed reactions. On the one hand, having been through so much with Garrett, I had confidence in his perceptions. We threw a party of celebration in his brain and invited all the white cells. We tossed rainbows all around inside his head, and we danced around with his white cells, saying "We did it! We did it!"

But the cautious therapist side of me had more reservations and skepticism, since there was at this time no objective proof. I couldn't be sure that this change in his imagery meant that his tumor was truly gone. After all, he was still a child; perhaps he was engaging in wishful thinking. Perhaps he was getting tired of constantly doing the visualizations. As I was later to learn, nothing could have been farther from the truth; doing imagery had become an intrinsic part of the way he interacted with his body and with his life.

A Defense System Against New Invaders

We switched the imagery at this point to emphasize the surveillance that he had been doing all along. He pictured his white cells as powerful, successful, and numerous, and as constantly patrolling every single part of his brain and body looking for *any* unwanted outside invaders such as cold germs, viruses, or bacteria. The white cells also searched for and destroyed any unwanted cells that his body might produce or might not need any more. He understood that the primary job of the white cells was to do a patrolling and mop-up job in his body, and he willingly entered into this visualization and made it a part of his regular practice.

During the winter, Garrett continued to improve symptomatically and functionally. He was able to go from his leg brace to high boots, and eventually from the high boots to tennis shoes, a source of much delight. He continued to do daily visualizations of his white cells performing a thorough surveillance job of his entire body and especially of his brain. He never again saw the tumor in his imagery. He believed that his tumor was gone. However, it became evident that he also desired objective confirmation of this. Since no further medical treatments were advised, it had been decided that there was no reason to subject him to the discomfort and anxiety of another CAT scan.

In February 1980, Garrett lost his balance and fell somewhat mysteriously. A CAT scan to check him out was considered but not undertaken. A few days later he fell down the stairs at home. His parents thought he might have briefly lost consciousness, although he said he heard everything that was going on but just could not move for a few moments. His parents called the doctor, and once again the decision was made not to do a CAT scan immediately but rather to watch him the next day to see if he showed any symptoms such as loss of consciousness or vomiting. Garrett went to school as usual, and after lunch he vomited. So he was taken for a CAT scan at last.

Garrett's pediatrician requested the CAT scan, but he was not there when it was made. The doctor who performed the scan told Sue, "I need to call Dr. Parman and Dr. Reymond and then I want to talk to you." Sue responded, "I need fifteen minutes to get my husband here first." The doctor said that would not be necessary, but Sue said, "Oh, yes it is very necessary!" She and Richard had an agreement to hear any significant news together. Sue then went to get Richard. She was very worried and did not want to hear any bad news alone.

When they were all there together, the doctor asked if Garrett had had surgery. He said there was no concussion, and the tumor was gone. All they could find was a pea-sized fragment of calcification—the "funny little white spot"! Sue said "Yes, okay," and then it dawned on her. She shot out of the chair, scaring the doctor, and shouted "Gone? Gone!!" The doctor said if he hadn't known better, he would have thought it was surgically removed.

Sue and Richard thanked him and said they were very

grateful for the news, and he said *he* was the one that was grateful for the opportunity to give them this news. He said they had made his day; it was not often that he was able to be the bearer of such wonderful tidings.

That night I received a telephone call from Garrett with the good news. Everyone was amazed, except Garrett and me, but I think both of us were relieved to have this concrete confirmation of what we already knew. When Garrett's mother brought him for his next appointment, she exclaimed in her exuberance that the radiation had not accomplished this miracle. Garrett had done it entirely with his visualization. Garrett interjected that he thought the radiation *had* helped him, because it softened up his tumor and made it easier for him to get it with his white cells. I was sure he was right.

WHY ME?

A True Story

by Garrett Porter

AUTHOR'S FOREWORD

This is the true story about the trivias and triumphs of my life. I would like it to inspire and influence people who want to be healthy in spite of problems. My story is for those who sometimes must ask, "Why Me?"

—Garrett Porter, 1985

I WILL PREVAIL

*I won't settle for just surviving
I will settle for prevailing,
overcoming all obstacles.
I have fought a war, and won.
I have seen death, and cried.
I have seen life, and felt joy.*

I will prevail.

—Garrett
1981

CONTENTS

CHAPTER ONE

The Beginning

When I was the age of nine, I was diagnosed as having a brain tumor. From then on I started a fight—a fight for life. This is the story of my life and my fight for life. It is written to encourage others, for everything I have done, others can do too.

I don't know how to start off my story because it's so exciting to be writing a book. I guess I should tell you a little bit about what I was like before I found out about the brain tumor. I was a normal kid—sometimes I was a little stinker—but I was a regular kid, nothing special. I want you to know that. Yes, I bothered people sometimes—'cause—you know—kids do. I was pretty wild. I would run around the house and play, like every ordinary nine-year-old. I like baseball and toys and models. I like to play with my friends, especially my friend David—David Rivers, that is. He's about my age, and we've played everything from Ship to Baseball together. He was my best friend then, and he still is. I think partly he helped me get through my troubled times. Mostly he helped just by being my best friend, sticking by me through all this.

I lived in Topeka, Kansas (I still do) with my Mom and Dad and my two dogs, Cinder and DumDum. We did not name DumDum that—we got her from my uncle and aunt, who were moving to an apartment and had to put her to sleep. We didn't want that, so we took her. She was already named DumDum.

Also, I lived with one cat, one Siamese cat, that is. His name was Ralph. He thought he ruled the whole house. That's all my family.

Right toward the end of the summer when I was nine (1978), I started limping and my arm got numb. I had been swimming a lot and I thought I had swimmer's arm. My Mom thought I was limping because I had hurt my leg and had got into that habit. My arm got worse and my limp didn't go away, so I was put in the hospital in September for tests. I had only been in fourth grade two or three weeks when that happened.

On the third day I was in the hospital, the doctor came in my room and asked my parents to step out in the hall for a minute. One of the other kids in the room said they might be talking about something bad. Of course I dismissed it and said, "Oh, no, I doubt that very much!" Much to my surprise, when the doctor came in he pulled up a chair and sat down beside my bed and said, "Garrett, you have something inside your skull. We're not sure what it is. We think it's a brain tumor but we're not sure." Then he got up, talked to my parents for a minute, and then left the room.

Well, that scared me! It really gave me the shivers down the spine. My parents and I talked about this and we decided to take one day at a time. I don't know what else we talked about—I've either forgotten or blocked it out of my mind. I didn't really know what a brain tumor was, so I wasn't so scared of what it could do to me.

Well, they ran more tests and then I stayed in the hospital for a few more days, and then I got to go home.

After I got home, I played a while with the things I got for presents and stuff. Then, while I was doing this, our next-door-neighbor came over with a present. It was a model of a Porsche. I thanked him and he went on his way. A few minutes later my Dad and I started to put it together. About when we were in the middle of making the model, I asked him if this thing can kill me. And he said yes. Well that *really* scared me. I was really frightened. But for some reason I didn't cry. I don't know why, but I just didn't cry. Well, I just went on doing what I wanted to do.

My Mom and Dad called people we knew, and I called my friends and told them about it. Some people were shocked. I think David was the most shocked of all, even

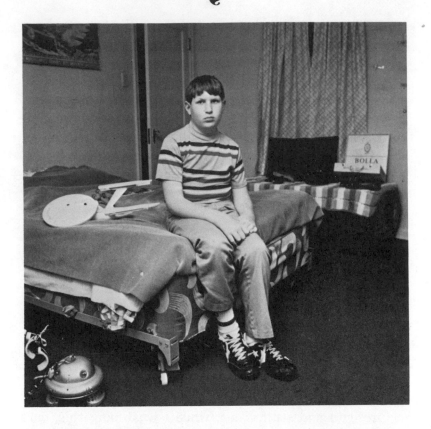

though he didn't show it. David was like Mr. Spock on *Star Trek*. He had no emotions at all. Well, at least it didn't *seem* like it to me at the time.

Later on, as time went on, David's emotions began to show. The way I knew this is because David started asking me questions. One day he asked me whether the tumor was malignant or benign—and things like that, whether I would get better and what would happen to me—and I could tell from his questions, and the way he asked, that he really cared about me. That was the beginning of my fight for life.

CHAPTER TWO

Facing Facts

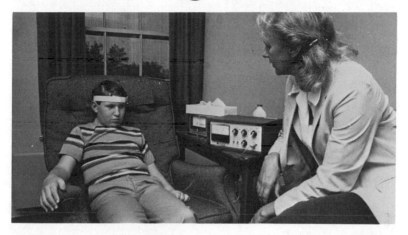

Over the next few months we started to take action, like radiation and biofeedback. The radiation treatment took place mostly in October of 1978. The radiation was performed at St. Francis Hospital in Topeka. The first time when I went in for treatment being radiated, I was more curious than I was scared. I wanted to see what the machine looked like. It turned out that you lay on a table that can be raised or lowered. There is a machine that is above you. It is moved into the right place by people that work in the Radiation Department. Then they turn it on for about a minute, and then they turn it off and move it into another position. Then they do the same thing over again. I think it lasted for three or four, actually six weeks. One thing I remember *very* well is that on Halloween day when I went there in the morning, I wore my Halloween costume, which was a mummy suit. My Mom made it, and I wore it to my radiation treatment and to Halloween.

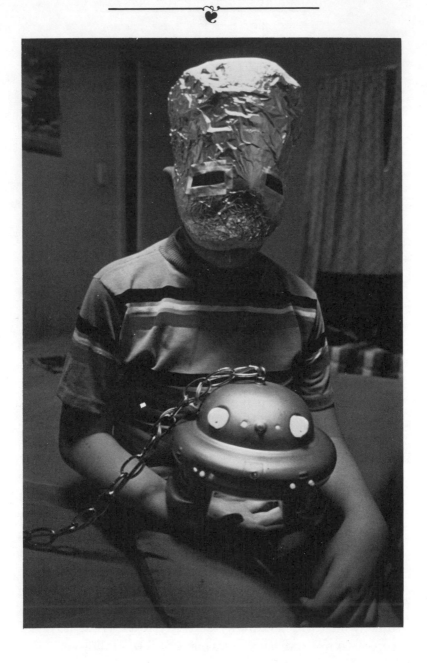

When my hair fell out, I felt that everybody was star-ing at me, that I was looked upon as weird and just teased. I hated that. Some people, really . . . I heard from my girlfriend Geraldine the other day, on Saturday. I asked her what she thought—people didn't think it was a wig, they thought it was a new hairstyle—except, the only one who thought it was a wig was Geraldine. She just knew.

Hawaii was one dream that wasn't met. During this time there were lots of triumphs and also disappointments. One of the big disappointments was going to Hawaii (al-though one thing I *did* enjoy seeing was Pearl Harbor and the *Arizona*). We started talking about a trip to Hawaii one night at the dinner table, but I never thought I'd get to go there. I remember I got hints, but I don't remember quite what was said. So, when my last present on Christmas was an airline ticket to Hawaii, I was really surprised. I had a hard time figuring out what it was at first—then I started getting excited. I was really looking forward to it. The plane trip was neat but—I'm not saying I don't like Hawaii—it just wasn't the right timing. I think it was mostly the fear of dying and everything, but when we got there I didn't feel good. The trip was really hard on every-body. I think this was because we were facing the fact that this possibly was our last trip together (now that turned out to be not true—'cause I lived—or else I wouldn't be sitting here in this chair writing this story), but anyway it was a relief to get home.

Eventually it was decided that I would have to have a brace, for how long we didn't know. It ended up being for about a year. The brace was to support my foot up in a position that allowed me to take a step without dragging my toe or tripping. I had trouble stepping, and we thought maybe that would work. I wore it for about a year, and then finally I was able to take it off. The day I could take it off I went to a shoe store and bought some boots—Dingo boots—and then we proceeded on to Stratton Hardware where we bought one sledge hammer. When we got home, I immediately called David Rivers and said, "Why don't you come over?" After he got to my house, we went downstairs with the sledge hammer and the brace. We each took turns beating the living daylights out of that brace. I remember so joyfully beating it until it was flat as a pancake. I remember clearly stating, "As long as I live I hope I never have to wear another brace!"

CHAPTER THREE

I Choose Life

*T*his is the part I'm going to *love* to do—my favorite part—cause I know the whole thing, *by heart!*

I think the most important decision in my lifetime was the decision between life or death. The decision between life or death was one that was going to be hard. I had to decide if I wanted to fight and risk the pain of it all and the agony, or give up without a fight. Well, I never was a quitter, and I decided I wasn't going to start then. My choice was life. It was going to be like a battle. I had to put out every force against this disease. I said to myself, "Dammit, I'm going to win this war against this disease." I went into battle with my white cells, my courage, and my faith. We waged war against the brain tumor, and I knew it was going to be a struggle, but I just decided I could not give up. So on and on and on, I fought day by day. The first visualization I had was of spaceships attacking my tumor. The whole battle was going on inside my brain. And I was winning over the tumor.

Pat (Norris) and I decided to make a cassette tape of my war with my tumor. I used the tape myself, but part of my idea was to make a tape that kids would like. Here is what we said on the tape.

(Note from Dr. Norris: In Garrett's visualization, his programming ego is portrayed by Blue Leader, the leader of a squadron of fighter planes. His brain is represented by the solar system, and his tumor is represented as an invading planetoid which is entering the solar system and threatening its existence. His white cells and other immune defenses are represented by the lasers and torpedoes with which the squadron of fighter planes is armed. In the taping, Garrett ran all the sound effects and also played the roles both of Blue Leader and a robotized computer in Blue Leader's plane. My role was Ground Control, and by this device we were able to maintain a constant dialogue on the tape. A transcription of the tape we made follows.)

(Sound effects from an electronic game ... beep ... beep ... after a minute, fade.)

Garrett: You are about to experience a method used for fighting tumors and cancer.
Pat: Command Post to pilot, Command Post to pilot. Get into your pilot suit. Take-off is in approximately ten minutes. Prior to take-off, it is very important to be in a completely relaxed state so that the battle will go its very best. Get into a comfortable position. Close your eyes. Wiggle out all the tensions you might feel in your

feet, legs, arms, chest. Wiggle your head. Now relax. Exhale and inhale *(loud exhalations and inhalations can be heard)* and exhale and inhale *(breathing sounds)*, and exhale *(breathing sounds)*. Now, forget breathing, and do your best to follow all the procedural instructions. Now, keeping your eyes closed, look at your feet with your mind's eye. Look at your feet with your mind's eye and curl up your toes. Relax your feet, and say *let go, relax.* Now, make mental contact with your legs. Tense up the muscles in your whole leg, and relax them. Relax them as completely as you can. Now, relax them again.

Garrett: Take-off in five minutes, Sir.

Pat: All right, pilots are following procedure on schedule. Now clench your fists and tense your hands as much as you can, and let go. Let relaxation seep into your palms, fingers, thumbs. Now, tense up your whole arm; let it feel really tense just for a moment, and then relax it. Relax, let go. Now become aware of your neck.

Allow the muscles that might be tense in your neck,
your throat, in your voice box to relax. For just a second, tense up your throat and relax. Let your whole
neck and throat relax, and now think of your face and
scalp. Make mental contact with your face and scalp.

Garrett: Take-off in three minutes, Sir.

Pat: We're proceeding very rapidly toward take-off time.
Take-off time is almost here. Now, clench your eyes really tight, screw up your face, tense all the muscles in
your face and scalp just for a second, hold it, and relax.
Relax completely.

Garrett: Fighter pilots to their planes. Fighter pilots to
their planes.

Pat: Yes, the planes and pilots are ready. All right, the relaxation has been accomplished, and the pilots are
ready to go, Sir.

(Sound effects left on throughout the entire dialogue, which follows.)

Garrett: Computers on. Computers on.

Pat: Roger.

Garrett: All fighter pilots should have their computers on.

Pat: All right, we are ready to take off. Now, imagine yourself taking hold of the controls, and be ready to go. *(Pause)* Blue Leader, Blue Leader, this is Command Post. Is all ready for take-off?

Garrett: A few more locking-in coordinates, Sir. *(Pause)*

Pat: Signal when ready.

Garrett: Ready, Sir.

This is a picture of how I visualized my
space battle, inside my brain.

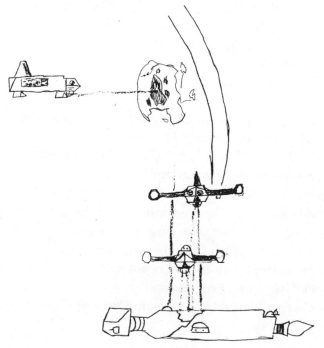

Pat: All right, ease in the throttle and take off. Let's keep in voice contact as you go. Your planes are rising nicely on the radar. It's approaching target. Now, as you get near, tell me what you see. Tell me when you see anything at all.

Garrett: I see some kind of round ball, Sir.

Pat: A round ball . . . do you think it's the target?

Garrett: Checking out in my calculator, Sir . . . calculators say that it's the target, Sir.

Pat: Excellent. Now describe what you see.

Garrett: It's a round-shaped . . . dumb-looking thing.

Pat: All right, prepare for attack. Ready laser gun number one. Ready laser gun number two. *(Sound effects)*

Garrett: Ready, Sir.

Pat: Now, fire!

Garrett: Firing, Sir. Commence firing, squadrons. *(Sound of missile, fades off with no explosion)* Missed, Sir!

Pat: All right, prepare to fire again. *(Sound effects)* Signal when ready.

Garrett: Ready, Sir.

Pat: Fire!

Garrett: Commence firing, squadron. *(Sound of missile being sent and hitting)* Hit, Sir!

Pat: A direct hit! A direct hit! Excellent, excellent! Do you see something dissolving?

Garrett: Yes, Sir. The side of the thing is dissolving.

Pat: Excellent! Let's have another attack now. Prepare laser gun number two. Fire when ready.

Garrett: We've got a jam up here, Sir.

Pat: What seems to be the problem?

Garrett: My guns are jammed!

Pat: Can you try laser gun number two?

Garrett: I'll try, Sir.

Pat: Fire when ready. *(Sound of missile being sent)*

Garrett: Missed, Sir!

Pat: All right, let's try laser gun number one again.

Garrett: Torpedo on stand-by, Sir.

Pat: All right, fire when ready. *(Sound of missile being sent)* Missed again! All right, let's bring up the laser gun from the rear.

Garrett: Yes, Sir. Bringing up laser gun from the rear. *(Beeping noise)* It's up, Sir.

Pat: Excellent. Prepare to fire.

Garrett: Preparing to fire.

Pat: Fire when ready. *(Sound of missile being sent and hit)* It's a hit! It's a hit! Describe what you see.

Garrett: It is not gone, but it is slowly going, Sir.

Pat: Excellent, Blue Leader, excellent! Are you in shape for another try?

Garrett: Yes, Sir.

Pat: All right, prepare laser gun number one.

Garrett: Preparing, Sir. *(Sound of missile being sent out)* Missed, Sir!

Pat: All right, let's have another successful attack here. Prepare the gun you brought up from the rear again.

Garrett: Yes, Sir. Bringing up from rear. It is jammed, Sir. I suggest missile hatch opening.

Pat: Excellent idea. Go ahead.

Garrett: Opening missile hatch, preparing missile to fire. *(Beeping sound)* A few more locking-in targets, Sir.

Pat: Proceed. Everything is under control. *(Sound of missile being sent)* Another miss! All right . . .

Garrett: Wait, Sir. It has knocked the side. It has blown a piece off.

Pat: Excellent, excellent! Watch it float away. Watch it float away and disintegrate.

Garrett: I will destroy it with my laser gun, Sir. *(Sound of missile being sent)*

Pat: Did that hit the side too?

Garrett: No, Sir.

Pat: All right, prepare whichever gun seems most ready now.

Garrett: I had better try loading the missiles up again.

Pat: Go ahead. Command Post to Blue Leader. Everything looks excellent from here. *(Sound of missile being sent)*

Garrett: It has knocked a piece off, Sir.

Pat: Excellent, excellent! Watch it dissolving now. Send in the white cell mop-up squad.

Garrett: Sending in white cell mop-up squad. Letting loose, Sir.

Pat: Excellent, excellent!

Garrett: That should be enough, Sir.

Pat: All right, prepare as previously. *(Sound of missile being sent)*

Garrett: Sir, they commenced firing at us, but . . . *(sound of missile being sent)* . . . nothing is hit, Sir!

Pat: All right, excellent! Put up shield! Put up shield! Tell computer to build ten times as many white cells. Contact computer.

Garrett: Contacting computer. Computer, do you read me? Computer, do you read me? *(Change of voice to play part of computer)* Computer hears. Computer hears. *(Garrett):* Send in twice as many white blood cells. *(Computer Voice):* I read. I read. *(Beeping noise)* Computer, stop. *(Beeping noise stops)*

Pat: Your shield looks in position. Your forces are well distributed around the perimeter. I would say we have an A-OK, go.

Garrett: Locking in with guns.

Pat: Signal when ready.

Garrett: Won't be ready for a few more minutes, Sir.

Pat: All right.

Garrett: Sir, we had a mix-up in firing.

Pat: What do you suggest, Blue Leader?

Garrett: Trying again, Sir.

Pat: Proceed.

Garrett: Ready for firing, Sir.

Pat: Fire on signal. Go!

Garrett: Yes, Sir. *(Sound of missile being sent and hitting)*

Pat: I have a direct hit on my screen! Confirm, please.

Garrett: Direct hit accomplished, Sir.

Pat: Excellent! Quite a bit should be dissolving off the sides from that. Can you see it?

Garrett: Yes, Sir.

Pat: Very good.

Garrett: Wait, Sir. There is an unknown ship heading directly for us.

Pat: All right, stand by to determine whether friend or foe.

Garrett: Computers are determining. *(Pause)* Computer, acknowledge, is that friend or enemy? Repeat—is that friend or enemy? *(Computer Voice):* Computer acknowledges that is a Malanium ship from that planet. It is an escape ship with many different people who can build another planet. My suggestions, Sir, are to, to, to—thank you, Sir,—to destroy. *(Garrett):* Thank you for your suggestion. I attached you into that. Did you hear it?

Pat: Yes, I could hear it. Well, perhaps we should follow the computer's suggestion.

Garrett: I've already begun. *(Sound of missile firing and hitting)*

Pat: Aha, Malanium ship. *(Beeping noise)* Interpret, please. Interpret, please.

Garrett: The Malanium ship is fully destroyed. No survivors, Sir.

Pat: Excellent, excellent. Let's remove all intruders if they appear. Now check white blood cell count.

Garrett: White blood cell scanning—scanning for white blood cells. Sir?

Pat: Yes, Blue Leader.

Garrett: They were shot down by enemy forces. No matter to worry, Sir. Make more of them.

Pat: Excellent idea. Make more at once. White blood cell capacity increases with increasing manufacture.

Garrett: Now hear this, computer. You are ordered to double the region you gave out before. Do you hear me—double it! *(Computer Voice):* I hear and obey, Sir. *(Garrett):* Something is wrong; they are not working. *(Computer Voice):* Sorry, Sir, but you have it on "Off." *(Garrett):* Don't get smart with me, computer. *(Beeping noise)* Stop right about now. *(Beeping noise stops)* Stand by for releasing shells with those body white cells in them.

Pat: Standing by.

Garrett: Countdown.

Pat: 10, 9.

Garrett: Loading, Sir.

Pat: Ready to load.

Garrett: Okay.

Pat: 5, 4, 3, 2, 1.

Garrett: Fire! Impact, will explode now. *(Sound of hitting)*

Pat: Another direct hit! Look at those white cells swarming.

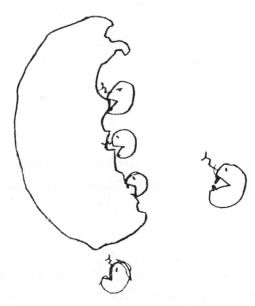

Garrett: They are eating away at it, Sir.

Pat: Excellent! Command Post to Blue Leader . . .

Garrett: Blue Leader, here, Sir.

Pat: It is time to return temporarily for refueling. Prepare to return to base for refueling.

Garrett: Returning to base for refueling, Sir. Come on, my squadron, head back home. Drinks on me.

Pat: Aha, I'm ready. Let me know when you have landed.

Garrett: Stand by for landing. Landing gear down. *(Beeping noise)* Landing gear is down, Sir.

Pat: Excellent battle, Blue Leader! I am glad you are standing for drinks. Now bring your awareness back into the relaxed state. Notice your feeling of well-being throughout your body. Gradually activate and descend. I am waiting for my drink.

Garrett: I didn't mean you, computer.

Pat: (Using computer voice): Well, I like it sometimes, too, you know.

Garrett: I know. Okay, a can of oil for you.

Pat: (Using computer voice): Thank you, Sir. Thank you, Sir.

I did it for over a year, and I remember so well because it was a real shock. I was doing my daily routine and the tumor just wasn't there. I couldn't find it at all. So I tried again, but I couldn't see it—and then I realized, it wasn't there!

It was so strange that night—I went up to bed, said my prayers and everything, and I was doing my visualization, and I couldn't find my tumor at all. It was just black, except for a tiny, white spot. I called and asked my Dad to come in, and I said I couldn't see it any more. He didn't believe it was gone, and we told Mom—but, maybe I wasn't concentrating, and I went through the relaxation again, did the imagery again—and still no tumor.

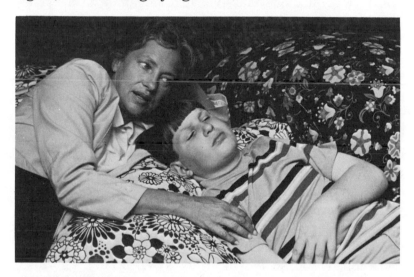

The next time I went to see my biofeedback doctor, Pat Norris, I told her I couldn't find my tumor. We did another imagery session right then, walking all through my brain together, but I couldn't find any sign of my tumor. So we celebrated, calling all the white cells to a party. We did a dance and said, "We did it, we did it" and threw rainbows around. Then we drew a picture of the celebration party together and put every color of the rainbow in it.

My next visualization—I still use—is my white cells like radar, turning, looking, communicating, "This is Section 3, Checking Section 3." They go everywhere, are always alert. This might be my visualization the rest of my life, or it might change some, who can say? A year of constant battling was over. In fact, I think the last attack was the biggest one of all. It seemed like it was a surprise attack—there was a *big rush* of all the men and white cells—a surprise attack that finally won out like good over evil. It was just one massive rush, engaging in a battle over, well, you could say, the dark side. The final conflict, and as we all know, I came out victorious.

About five months later I fell down the stairs and had seemed okay at that time, so I went on to eat dinner. The next day at school, I threw up or upchucked or however you want to put it. My Mom came and got me and took me to the hospital. She said, "You'll probably have to have another CAT scan," and I said, "It's a waste of time, Mom, they won't be able to confirm anything." When I had CAT scans, they couldn't tell if the tumor was growing, or shrinking, or what—so—I thought I was going to have another check-up on the tumor, but it turned out that it was a check-up to see if I had a concussion. The doctor feared I had a concussion, so he sent me for a CAT scan. I went into the room for a CAT scan.

I think I should explain about what a CAT scan is. The room held a large machine. There is a kind of a table there and you get on this—not really a table and not really a bed—you're lying down, and it's kind of a bed. It slides out and you get on it and then it slides back in. It sounds like a washing machine. Your head goes into it, and this round cylinder slides right into it, and your head is inside this machine, and this cylinder goes around your head, and it's taking pictures. It goes around and takes pictures for about twenty minutes and then stops and goes the other way for about twenty minutes. Then when it stops they give you a shot of some dye, and it starts up again and the cylinder goes around each way for about twenty minutes, taking pictures again.

The pictures are x-rays of cross-sections of your whole

head and skull and brain, many cross-sections of each part of your head. These pictures show my CAT scan before and after the tumor was gone. It really isn't too scary. They explained it, everything that was going to happen. Also, there's an intercom in there so you can talk to the operators, or ask if you need anything. Of course, I *hated* the shot. I can bear it, but it's not one of my favorite things. I don't think it's *anyone's* favorite thing. You could call me needle shy. Could, hah! *Can* call me needle shy.

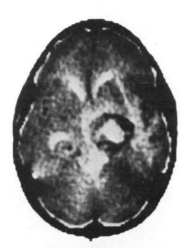
February 1979

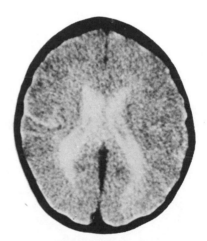
February 1980

As I remember it, I got out and the girls who were running it asked me if I wanted a candy bar, and I thought that was really neat. They ran down and got it for me and gave it to me. Then I went out in the waiting room where my Mom was waiting. We waited about five minutes and the doctor came into the waiting room and my Dad had just arrived. They sat down, and the doctor told us that as far as a concussion was concerned, I was fine—and that the tumor was gone. And my Mother jumped up and shouted, "The tumor is gone?" and scared the doctor half to death.

We talked a few minutes. I remember going home and calling all my friends, including Pat, to tell them the tumor was *gone*!!! I felt relieved, and I felt proud, and most of all, I felt triumphant, because—you know—I *did* beat it. I was really, really glad; I was overjoyed. I guess that's what I can remember most. When the tumor was gone, I popped through the clouds.

CHAPTER FOUR

There Is a Rainbow Behind Every Dark Cloud

*O*ne of the people who helped me with my brain tumor was Jerry Jampolsky. Jerry runs a center out in Tiburon, California. It's called the Center for Attitudinal Healing. I heard about Jerry when Pat gave me the book, *There is a Rainbow Behind Every Dark Cloud,* written by some of the kids at the Center. I first met him by a telephone call. I was at my biofeedback lessons, at Menninger's, and Pat called him for me to see if I could be on his "hotline." I got to talk with Jerry Jampolsky and became a phone pal. Here's what happened. (I don't want to put in that part about CBS and all because it makes me sound like too much—I've been on TV and all that junk.) As I began to get in touch with other kids, and I helped other kids also, I began to get more and more involved. Then, I started my own hotline. I called the hotline "Kids Help Hotline." I had a special telephone number, and I still do.

The first phone pal I met (on my own hotline) was Terri Oberdine. When I first met her she was eighteen years old. Terri and I got to know each other real well. Terri is a very kind, caring human being. Not only did we have fun together, like going to the movies or going bowling, but we became a team. We would visit kids in the hospital and at their homes who had life-threatening illnesses. The first person we visited was a boy named Eric Bossey. He had just had an operation on his brain tumor. So, naturally his hair was shaved off, and he was partly bald. He was a little bit embarrassed, and Terri and I could understand that very well. On our first visit, we talked for a while and then we had to go home. About a week later, we invited Eric to go to the zoo with us. He accepted, and we went on Saturday. Terri had her own car so it was easy for us to do this on our own. We had a lot of fun and said we'd take him back some time.

———————————❦———————————

We visited Eric several more times. About a few months later, Eric was back in the hospital. We went to visit him one night, and he was feeling pretty poorly. He was really pretty sick. He couldn't eat anything because he would upchuck it. We stayed there a while and talked to him, but he was really out of it. He would just shake his head. Well, that night we left, and a few days later Eric died. In a way, that was worse than having the brain tumor. I had Terri to talk to; that was nice. I went to his funeral, cried my eyes out, and I still miss him. You get so close to people when you share something so deep with them. I'm real close to Terri. In one way, they're closer than your real relatives.

Well, after that we recovered, and Terri and I went on. We had other contacts on the phone, and about last year we met a girl, about nine or ten, who had cancer, and her name's Michele. We talk with her like we did with Eric. I haven't seen her for more than a month. She's doing fine, going back and forth to the Kansas University Medical Center. She's taking chemotherapy, and she's doing okay. We still have our partnership going and our hotline going, and we will keep on doing this work.

Conclusion

Before I explain the answer to "Why Me?" I want to say it wasn't an easy thing—I had to work and work and work—and that's what I want to stress most of all, it was *no* piece of cake. If I don't stress *that,* some people might think, "Boy, you're incredible." No, that's not true. It may have been miraculous, but anybody can do it, though it's a lot of work and constant attention, and it was exhausting at times.

I'd like to answer the question, "Why Me?" I guess there is no one answer. I feel I may have been tested by the Lord, or it just could have been a coincidental thing. But it just goes to show you, you can do anything that you want if you just try hard enough.

If I had my choice, in spite of all my excitement and being on TV and all, I'd choose to be like I was before I knew I had the tumor and I didn't even limp. I wish I could take a time trip and see what that would be like. I'd also like to take a time trip into my future to see what that would be like. But if I had my choice, I'd be regular and this wouldn't have happened.

Garrett's drawings of his Visualizations

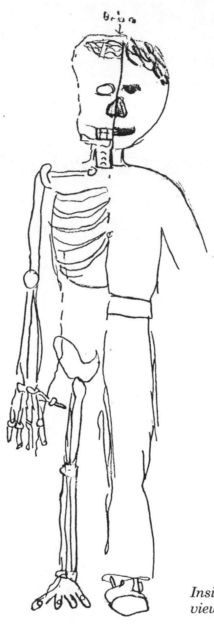

*Inside and outside
view of my body*

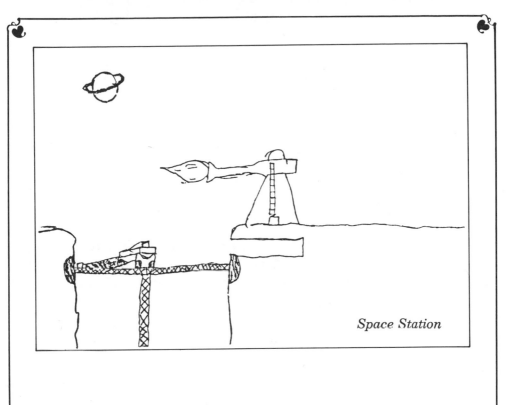

Space Station

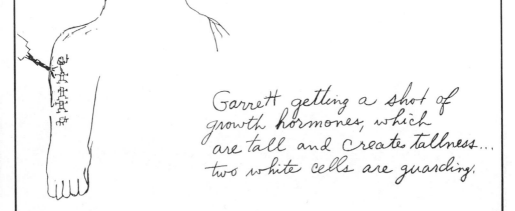

What's That Feeling?

Garrett getting a shot of
growth hormones, which
are tall and creates tallness...
two white cells are guarding.

The spirit is the master, imagination the tool, and the body the plastic material . . . The power of the imagination is a great factor in medicine. It may produce diseases in man and in animals, and it may cure them . . . Ills of the body may be cured by physical remedies or by the power of the spirit acting through the soul.

—PARACELSUS, FATHER OF MODERN MEDICINE

CHAPTER THREE

Dynamics Of Visualization And Imagery In Therapy

In ancient and modern times, in both East and West, visualization has with few exceptions enjoyed an illustrious history. It has been a cornerstone of many healing methods.

The earliest visualization techniques ever recorded are from Babylonia and Sumaria. Histories of all peoples, from ancient Egypt and Babylonia through the middle ages and right up to modern times, include accounts of healing, and these all incorporate visualization in one form or another. The modern exception, which until very recently influenced *our* conceptions of healing, occurred in the early part of this century when behaviorist John Watson called imagery "bunk" and relegated it to "psychology's dead past." Now imagery and visualization are becoming important and influential once again. In 1964 Robert Holt offered a strong argument in favor of imagery research in his article, "The

Return of the Ostracized." Now many psychologists are recognizing imagery and visualization as among the most powerful tools in cognitive psychology.

From the famous healing temples of ancient Greece to present-day pilgrims traveling to Mecca and Lourdes, from the Hermetic rites to help a person visualize himself in perfect health to modern day Christian Science, visualization has been employed as a powerful tool for inner change.

Early uses of visualization in healing were based on a religious or mystical tradition, permeating the thought of the mystery schools including the Hermetic, the Essenes, the Platonic philosophers, and later the Rosicrucians, the Kabbalists, and Gnostic Christians. All had in common a belief in the primacy of spirit over matter, of mind over body. They believed that matter was a manifestation of mind. Many modern thinkers express the same belief. Swami Rama, in explaining his ability to control his heart rate, blood flow, and other physical processes stated, "All of the body is in the mind, but not all of the mind is in the body." Ayurvedic medicine, the Swami's tradition, had, from ancient to modern times, as its real purpose, the development of consciousness rather than simply the healing of disease.

The modern Indian philosopher, Sri Aurobindo, has stated that you can think of spirit as the subtlest form of matter, or you can think of matter as the densest form of spirit. Physical bodies, emotions, thoughts, and spirit are all interpenetrating energy structures in Sri Aurobindo's system. This is also the basic position put forth in the Yoga Sutras of Patanjali, dating back to the second century before Christ.

On this continent, initiates of the Midewiwin, or Grand Medicine Society of the Ojibwas, were instructed in healing and in directing the forces moving through the vital centers of the human body through visualizations. In modern times, American Indian medicine men such as Rolling Thunder, reported on by Doug Boyd in his book of that title, evoke the powers of the mind in healing the body through visualizations.

Among the forty-two books of Hermes, considered to be the earliest-known founder of the art of healing, there are six which are medical, classified as the Pastophorus or "image-bearers." In the middle ages, Paracelsus (1493-1541) devoted his entire life to the study of Hermetic healing. Many remarkable cures are ascribed to him. Although the medical fraternity of the times maligned him, he was adored by the masses and extolled on his tombstone: "Here lies buried Philip Theophastus the famous Doctor of Medicine who cured Wounds, Leprosy, Gout, Dropsy and other Incurable Maladies of the Body, with wonderful Knowledge and gave his goods to be divided and distributed to the Poor."

The Essenes, early Christian mystics who are considered the progenitors of modern Freemasonry, were also healers of this order. According to Manly Palmer Hall, the name "Essene" is derived from an ancient Syrian word meaning "physician." The Essenes are believed to have held as their purposes of existence the healing of mind, soul, and body.

Visualization in Modern Cancer Therapy

Among the many modern uses of imagery in healing, both in psychotherapy and in physical medicine (Freud, Jung, Leuner, DeSoille, Assagioli, Wolpe, Lazarus, Jacobs,

Schultz and Luthe, Green and Green, Gerard), the use of imagery and visualization in cancer therapy is a relative newcomer. Carl and Stephanie Simonton are pioneers in this field, and in their now well-known book, *Getting Well Again: A Step-by-Step Self-Help Guide to Overcoming Cancer for Patients and their Families,* they describe how they decided to use visualization. They state:

> *From our study of biofeedback we learned that certain techniques were enabling people to influence their own internal body processes, such as heart rate and blood pressure. An important aspect of biofeedback, called visual imagery, was also a principal component of other techniques we had studied. The more we learned about the process, the more intrigued we became. Essentially, the visual imagery process involved a period of relaxation, during which the patient would mentally picture a desired goal or result. With the cancer patient, this would mean his attempting to visualize the cancer, the treatment destroying it and, most importantly, his body's natural defenses helping him recover. After discussions with two leading biofeedback researchers, Drs. Joe Kamiya and Elmer Green, of the Menninger Clinic, we decided to use visual imagery techniques with cancer patients.*

The Simontons taught patients to visualize their cancer cells or tumors as accurately as possible. They taught them that cancer cells are weak and mixed up, disorganized, and instilled confidence that bodies could naturally and normally defend against cancer. They also explained the treatment and its desired outcome, and they taught patients to visualize it as powerful and effective, capable of producing a positive outcome. Most importantly, they encouraged patients to develop visualizations of their white blood cells as being numerous and powerful, attacking and destroying the cancer.

Jeanne Achterberg and G. Frank Lawlis developed a diagnostic test to evaluate the effectiveness of cancer patients' imagery as a means of assessing their prognosis. After a brief relaxation, patients were asked to image their cancer, their immune system, and their medical treatment, and to draw a picture of each of them. Patients were then interviewed in a structured interview. By these means, their unconscious imagery—their beliefs about their cancer and their ability to get well—were elicited.

They were able to isolate fourteen factors which seem to have high prognostic value, involving vividness, activity, and strength of the cancer cells; vividness, activity, and strength of the white blood cells; and the relative size and numbers of white cells as compared to cancer cells. Other important factors were vividness and strength of the medical treatment being received, the overall strength of the imagery, and the emotional investment of the patient.

With respect to the last of the fourteen factors, clinical judgment, they note several characteristics which seem to be predictors of positive health which could not be validated statistically since so few cases share commonalities. These include a continuity of symbolism, that is, symbols in context with each other and integrated into a single perception; those symbols that have a high degree of emotional value attached to them; and the degree to which the person appears to maintain the symbol as a continuous source of comfort or support, e.g., "My watchdogs are usually looking after me," or "My body warriors are at watch *always.*"

This internal experience of *constancy*, of perfect functioning, is a very important one. When Garrett was dictating his own story to me, I was very impressed by the way in which he told of the surveillance of his body by his white cells. He described how they checked "each quadrant" of his brain, making sure all areas were free of cancer cells or other troublesome invaders, and then he said "and this is the visualization I may do for the rest of my life." He paused for a moment and then he said thoughtfully, ". . . or, it may change some, who knows?" The depth of wisdom in this is amazing, both in terms of the matter-of-factness with which he contemplated visualizing for the rest of his life and in terms of his recognition of the natural evolution of images.

Another child I worked with, a delightful five-year-old boy from another city, also had had a brain tumor. After hearing Garrett's tape and having as clear a description as possible, in terms he could understand, of what his immune system "inside his skin" could do for him, John drew a picture of himself and his white cells. He had decided that his white cells would be "The Incredible Hulk," and in his picture, he had a simple orange stick-figure person in the middle of the sheet and two green stick-figures, one on each side, each with an arm sticking straight out over the orange figure. He explained, ". . . these Incredible Hulks are my white cells. They have their arms around me."

Toward A Deeper Understanding of Visualization and Imagery

Since the imagery a person holds of the disease process or of the healing process can affect the outcome of the illness to *any* extent, the question can be asked, *how* is the imagery related to the condition of the body? Does the imagery precede the condition, influencing or even causing it? Or does it simply reflect the condition as it exists? And if so, why is it so much a predictor of outcome, regardless of or separate from severity of disease?

Asking questions like these is like asking the famous old question, *which came first, the chicken or the egg?* The point of the question is, of course, to point out that they do not come separately; every chicken contains eggs, and every egg contains a chicken. They are both a part of a process of *being* and *becoming.* This is exactly the relationship between body imagery and the condition of the body.

Carl and Stephanie Simonton were impressed by this relationship evidenced by biofeedback. In their book, *Getting Well Again,* they write,

> *Elmer and Alyce Green ... believe that biofeedback techniques have clearly demonstrated the principle that,* "Every change in the physiological state is accompanied by an appropriate change in the mental emotional state, conscious or unconscious, and conversely, every change in the mental emotional state, conscious or unconscious, is accompanied by an appropriate change in the physiological state." *In other words, mind, body, and emotions are a unitary system—affect one and you affect the others.*

In our work with cancer patients, biofeedback plays an immensely important role, not only for all of its good effects on reducing stress, pain, anxiety, and fear, but especially because it provides indispensable *experiential* evidence of mind controlling body, of visualizations influencing physical processes. It is not a question of *believing* that mind can affect healing, but of *knowing* from the inside that this is true.

In starting out, it is important and necessary to analyze the individual's own conscious and unconscious imagery regarding what is presently occurring in their body. Recently there have been many attempts to create ready-made visualizations on video or audio cassettes. But I believe that "canned" imagery can only be of limited value, according to how well it matches the person's own unconscious belief and knowledge about what is actually happening inside his own body. An important part of self-regulation is development of one's own individual visualization, using internal symbology which has deep unconscious meaning for the individual.

It is fascinating to see evidence of unconscious knowledge of the state of the body. Patients often have dreams about a condition long before symptoms have brought it to their conscious attention or before a diagnosis is made. Carl G. Jung was expert at translating the dream symbols into diagnoses, even when the imagery was obscure. A dream may speak organically both before and after the emergence of bodily disturbance. Dreams do not merely provide information about the psychological situation of the dreamer but may also disclose the presence of organic disorder and even denote its precise location. Two other researchers of psychotherapeutic work with cancer patients, Meredith Sabini and Valerie Hone Maffly, followed the dreams of cancer patients and observed how closely their dreams followed the course of their illness.

Although I occasionally use dreams of patients in my work, in general I prefer to use active imagination by means of guided imagery trips into the body and through drawings. The results of these exploration trips are sometimes immediately confirmed.

One of my patients, for example, injured his back and was in considerable pain. We made an appointment for him with an osteopath. Since the appointment was several hours away, and his discomfort was interfering with the other work we were doing, I decided to have him take a trip down his spine, with the intent of relaxing his paraspinal muscles, thereby increasing circulation and reducing pain. As he moved down his spine in his image, he got a clear mental picture of the third lumbar disk slipped out to the left, and this image was exactly confirmed later that afternoon by X-ray. This occurrence served as confirmation for him of the close connection between his mental and physical processes.

Another person, during a psychosynthesis class in which we were doing "Dialogue with the Body," received such a clear image of her pancreatic duct that she was able to go to an anatomy book and then to her doctor with this image and thus provide the clue that led to the correct diagnosis of a condition that had been defying identification for more than two years.

Garrett had two instances of *seeing* inside his body when he was completely relaxed. One was that first evening when, finding him tumor gone, he beheld instead that "funny little white thing." His second experience of this occurred when he was working with his pituitary, which, following radiation, no longer had the capacity to produce growth hormone. While deeply relaxed, he suddenly *saw* this gland as clearly as if he were looking with his eyes open.

Experiences of this kind are certainly interesting, and countless anecdotes of this sort abound. More often than not, there is no immediate confirmation of the anatomical accuracy of these investigative images. There can be little doubt, however, that they have symbolic meaning to the individual, and this is the basis on which we begin.

Gradually, through a process of visualization and imagery, a bridge is built between conscious and unconscious processes, which includes cortical and subcortical processes, the conscious and "unconscious" portions of the brain. Evidence is mounting as to neurohumoral and biochemical mechanisms whereby this can take place.

No uniform terminology exists, but I want to distinguish between *visualization* and *imagery* in the following way. *Visualization* is the consciously chosen, intentional instruction to the body. *Imagery* is the spontaneously occurring "answer," qualifier and modifier from the unconscious. Thus, a two-way communication is set up by the interplay of visualization and imagery.

The relationship between visualization and imagery can be thought of as a metaphor, as the relationship between a transmitter and a receiver. The visualization acts as a message *to* the unconscious, including the subcortical parts of the brain and particularly the limbic system, hypothalamus, and pituitary. The images are messages *from* the unconscious to consciousness, much as dreams are.

This is beautifully illustrated in the transcription of Garrett's abstract visualization. His consciously-chosen visualization was that he would destroy his tumor with lasers and torpedoes. During the course of making the tape, spontaneous imagery occurred when he suddenly proclaimed that another unidentified object was entering the solar system. He identified this as a spaceship containing creatures which could build another planetoid like the tumor he presently had. It was clear that this expressed his fear, perhaps entirely unconscious, that he might generate another tumor inside his brain. I recognized this from many other instances of working with visualizations and imagery, and when we were done with our taping session, I remarked to him that it must be scary to think that he could get another tumor. The relief that washed over his face on hearing this interpretation was clear evidence that something of considerable importance was being handled. This was an unconscious and quite possibly repressed fear that was very important for him to bring into consciousness and recognize that it could be managed by him in the same way that he was working on his other tumor.

Over a period of time, through an educative process, through asking the body what needs to be done, consulting the "inner physician," and through the psychotherapeutic processes, images are modified, if necessary, to become more productive of the results desired. This is the process of building a visualization, and usually, especially with adult patients, it is an ongoing process.

The rare but spectacular phenomenon of spontaneous remission of cancer patients persists in the annals of medicine, . . . a fascinating mystery, but at the same time a solid basis for hope in the future: if several hundred patients have succeeded in doing this sort of thing, eliminating vast numbers of malignant cells on their own, the possibility that medicine can learn to accomplish the same thing at will is surely within reach of imagining.

—*LEWIS THOMAS*

CHAPTER FOUR

Personalized Therapy

*I*n developing an effective visualization, one must consider a number of qualities, especially a *positive image*. In *Imagery of Cancer,* Achterberg and Lawlis state: "The symbols of positive connotation are those representing strength and purity; powerful enough to subdue an enemy—pure enough to do so with justification. Such images are frequently knights or ... Vikings— heroes only slightly removed in time and place from the white knights. The knight is an archaic symbol from fairy tales in which most of us have a common exposure."

A second quality of the visualization that I have found to be essential is that it must be *ego-syntonic;* that is, it must conform with the person's deepest desires and values. An excellent illustration of this point comes from a young woman who consulted me when I was giving a lecture in Phoenix, Arizona. She had a cancer growing against her cervical spine, pressing against the spinal cord. This was causing gradual loss of the use of her arm and immobility of her head and neck. It was growing in spite of medical treatment and also in spite of a program of biofeedback and visualization which she was following faithfully and in which she had invested effort and positive expectation. She was following a sound nutritional plan, exercising, doing everything she could to increase her health. In spite of all these things, her condition had deteriorated to the point where her physician had told her that she should prepare a will and prepare for the care of her two young daughters. She had been given only a few months to live.

She told me that her visualization just didn't seem to be working, and she wasn't sure why. She was visualizing her cancer as a dragon and her immune system as white knights attacking the dragon, but the knights never really seemed to be effective.

I asked her to draw a picture of her imagery. She drew a picture of white knights and a dragon that seemed pretty ordinary to me, but when she looked at her own drawing, she gasped and said, "Oh, my God, that's my husband." Her eyes filled with tears, and she said, "I can't kill my husband."

Her story unfolded. She was separated from her husband, an alcoholic who abused her and her daughters when he was drunk. She had been forced to leave him. She believed that the strain, tension, and sorrow of this situation, as well as the ensuing loss of the relationship, were the precipitating causes of her cancer. In other words, she believed that her husband was the dragon on her back.

In this case, only a simple reframing of her visualization was necessary. When she said that she could not kill her husband, I responded that it was not her husband that she needed to be rid of but rather the qualities and events that had caused her pain. It was the drunkenness and the abuse that needed to be symbolically eliminated.

If by means of this imagery she could eliminate these qualities from her husband, he would not only be unharmed, but he would be better off. And she could at least get these painful occurrences off her back, since they were the dragons she needed to release. Her eyes lit up at this suggestion, and she exclaimed enthusiastically, "Oh, the abuse, I can *really* kill the abuse."

The next time I saw her was a year later when I returned to the same annual conference in Phoenix to present a workshop. She told me that with this new perspective on her visualization, she had been able to put everything she had into it, and soon her tumor began to melt away. She was now in complete remission. She told this story to the workshop attendees, adding much to their experience and helping to make this point memorable: the visualization must be something that you are *willing* to do.

There are frequent variations on this theme among patients, the most common being that if their white cells are good, they can't kill or do harm. Patients also frequently identify in some way with their cancerous cells. It is essential not to simply ignore such issues. The patient must be helped to resolve them in a satisfactory way.

Tommy is another champion. When Tommy and I began his psychophysiologic therapy, he was eleven and one-half years old and had stage IVB Hodgkin's Disease. He had been diagnosed and staged the first time when he was nine years old. At that time Tommy's disease was IA, the least serious stage of Hodgkin's. As treatment progressed, Tommy's disease also progressed, to stage IVB. He had not responded to chemotherapy so far, and life was becoming pretty tough for him.

The time I first met him, Tommy had begun to try to

solve his very great problems by setting fires and other acting-out behavior. He was referred by David Berland, M.D., a child psychiatrist who was seeing Tommy and his family for formal family therapy.

Tommy had already been through much agony, including laparectomies, radiation and chemotherapy, pneumonia, chicken pox, and shingles. He had also had his spleen and appendix removed. He hated needles and injections, of which he had a great many. Now he was contemplating another course of treatment, a "sandwich" of chemotherapy, radiation, and chemotherapy. He wasn't sure he wanted to go through with it all, and in some ways he wanted to "burn his world down" instead.

The week Tommy was referred to me, Garrett was on a panel with Dr. Jerry Jampolsky and children who had recovered or were recovering from cancer. Jerry talked about the Center for Attitudinal Healing telephone network, and Garrett also told about his own hotline in Topeka. When the program was over, I saw Tommy go up to the front and speak with Garrett for a few minutes, and I assumed that he was asking Garrett for the hotline telephone number. A couple of weeks later, I asked Garrett if Tommy had called him and he said no, that Tommy had asked him for his autograph! I thought this strange at first, but later I realized the significance of it. Tommy considered Garrett a role model.

From the very beginning, Tommy worked intensely on all of the self-regulation skills. Since he was going through so much when we started, the first thing I showed him was the breathing exercises, believing they would help him get through the initial rough times more quickly than anything else. The second time he came, he sat down in the chair and immediately began the deep, calm, slow breathing so effectively that it was clear he had been practicing and practicing. He attended to everything earnestly and with the greatest concentration and seriousness.

Like Garrett, Tommy had to come to grips with whether he wanted to live or die. For him, the struggle took place on a more symbolic level. He identified with his cancer cells and felt they were being "scapegoated" and were trying to protect themselves. The drawings he made during the course of his therapy, especially following visualization sessions, were very revealing and useful to both of us in uncovering a number of unconscious attitudes. At one point, he imaged his cancer cells as hiding behind a lead shield that had been made to protect his liver during radiation treatments. He said, "They are just trying to survive like everybody else."

Tommy now explains that his belief that the cancer cells were hiding was reinforced by the fact that the cancer had always come back or had never been completely eliminated in the previous treatments. Eventually, he was able to realize that his cancer cells were on a self-destructive course and could not survive no matter what; the only question was whether or not they would destroy Tommy in the process.

Tommy was as intent as he could be on getting well, and he faithfully followed all the instructions and guidelines. He learned to like salads, grains, and vegetables, and reduced his intake of meat, sugar, and fried foods. He became very good at the self-regulation skills and enjoyed working with the biofeedback equipment as a result of the control he could demonstrate. He used these skills in a number of ways: to relax, to enhance his performance in sports, and to enhance his visualizations. And as was the case with Garrett, his parents were very supportive of all the things he was doing to heal himself. Although there was much stress, Tommy and his family confronted problems with love and openness.

As treatment progressed, a number of experiences served to build Tommy's confidence. Although previously he had hated his treatments and often resisted the chemotherapy through fighting and fear, he now used his new-found relaxation and imagery skills to remain calm. He became a model patient and was very pleased that he could handle things so well. He visualized the treatment as "coming into the neighborhood of his body like the army or the national guard, ready to mop up all the trouble makers." He became a great deal more serene. Although he had missed a lot of school in the beginning of the year, he managed to get caught up with his work and was justifiably proud of that.

Things were going much better for Tommy by the time the radiation phase of his treatment was to begin. He was looking forward to it with happy anticipation. During the chemotherapy, he had been wearing a heparin lock (a small shunt inserted into his vein and taped securely, holding the vein open for the repeated injections he would need) and could hardly wait to have it removed. He was an active and macho kid, and he was anxious to play football and engage in the rough and tumble play of his age group without always having to be careful of the shunt in his forearm.

So he was extremely disappointed to be told that the radiation would make him quite sick, that he would vomit and have diarrhea, and that he should eat meat and cheese and avoid vegetables and fruit. His mother told me that he was very upset. I decided to call Carl Simonton to see what he might suggest.

Carl said that the reaction that had been described was

at one end of a continuum of reactions to full-body radiation. Responses can range from almost no adverse reaction at all to the kind of reaction that had been described to Tommy. He suggested that since Tommy was good at self-regulation, he could just observe his body objectively, like a scientist, to see what his own reaction would be. Then, if he wanted to modify his reactions, he could work on them like he was working on all the other things he had been doing. As for his diet, the foods suggested were binding and would help if he had a lot of diarrhea. Otherwise, he could eat as he had been, and all the better for him.

Tommy was reassured to hear this and delighted to think that I had called Dr. Simonton on his behalf. These suggestions made sense to him because he had been able to tolerate the chemotherapy so much better this time, experiencing few adverse side effects. He knew that this was because of the control he was exercising within himself.

Before the radiation could be undertaken, a shield had to be made to protect his liver. When the shield was completed, there was a picture-taking session to assure that the liver was completely covered by the shield. Tommy thought that this process was actually his first radiation treatment. When it was finished, he told his Dad that it wasn't bad at all. His Dad replied that it was no wonder, since they were just taking pictures to be sure his liver was completely covered. About half an hour later, on the way home, Tom remarked to his father, "It's a good thing you told me they were only taking pictures, because otherwise I'd be getting sick about now." Then he smiled, chagrined, realizing the power of his mind in that a *negative placebo* was causing that queasy feeling until he remembered that he had not had radiation.

This was an important realization. After that, he sailed

through the radiation with few adverse side effects. He did play football and other sports, and he did eat whatever he wanted to, including his good nutritional diet, without discomfort.

During the next phase of chemotherapy, he continued to do well and feel better. His imagery was becoming powerful, and his confidence was growing all the time. He was doing fine in school and at home, and he was doing very well with his self-regulation and his visualizations. He decided to visualize growing hair every day, and his hair began to get thick and curly again.

In May 1981, just before school let out, the course of treatment was completed, and he went to the hospital for re-staging. The plan had been to do another laparectomy, a procedure of opening an incision from collar bone to groin to visually inspect and biopsy the lymph nodes and other tissues on one side of the body. He had already had three of these procedures, which he called his zippers. This time, he did not want that test, and his parents backed him up. The medical team then decided that they might be able to do a needle biopsy of his liver, although he was much younger than patients usually considered suitable. He would need to be awake for the procedure and fully cooperative, holding his breath when told to do so, even though there would be some pain with the procedure. Tommy thought he could do it, and because he had been doing so well during his other treatments, the staff agreed.

He came through the biopsy with flying colors. After the procedure, the doctors told him he behaved better than most adult patients. The results of the liver biopsy revealed no abnormalities. The next day he had a CT scan of his chest, abdomen, and pelvic area, with no evidence of the disease. He was in complete remission.

Now, four years later, Tommy is still in remission and

has just completed a physical examination giving him a clean bill of health.

When I finished sharing with Tommy the text I had written about him for the book, he added the following comment. He said that at first he had rebelled so much against the treatments, but after understanding something about voluntary control, he stopped struggling and just let everything happen. He said,

> *One thing I don't think they put enough emphasis on is the need for understanding and the importance of helping a patient release the anger. I believe the mind is what cured me, but anger swelled up in me from my cancer, and all the effort was on making me physically better. There was no relief from the anger. It was, "Well, we have to help you live!" It's harder for a young kid to have a clear concept of what you're doing with the chemotherapy. In biofeedback I knew what we were doing to get the mind over the cancer. It was a painful but growing experience. Now I think in terms of living a lifetime.*

Another important attribute of the visualization is that it be *felt* to be taking place inside the body. In other words, the imagery must be *kinesthetic* and *sensory* as well as visual. Although Garrett's imagery was a battle in outer space, he felt and visualized it taking place inside his head, literally as well as figuratively. The internalization of the imagery must take place, and usually this is accomplished fairly easily by the first "guided imagery" trips through the body. Occasionally people are unwilling or afraid to look inside. If possible, they must be helped to do so, and various techniques, similar to those used in systematic desensitization, can be employed.

Warts: Demonstration of the Need for Anatomical Accuracy in Visualization

A frequently-asked question is whether the visualization needs to be accurate. As has already been demonstrated, the visualization can be completely symbolic. In fact, often when a patient tries to be biologically accurate and tries to know exactly what is going on from a scientific and technical point of view, he only becomes frustrated. Nevertheless, it seems that the visualization does have to be *anatomically correct.*

I would like to illustrate this with an experience in self-healing of my own. A few years ago, I was bothered by a callous-like growth on the bottom of my foot. I thought it was a corn. I remember being bothered with it at Thanksgiving and at Christmas and later at some spring conferences that I attended. I remember these times specifically, because I had to take this corn into account and bring corn plasters and protective pads with me.

My foot was becoming more and more painful. I even tried to use solutions that are supposed to dissolve corns, and several times I went after it with clippers. Of course, I was also using visualization, seeing the skin growing smooth and firm beneath the corn, and also simply seeing it drying up and falling off. All of this was to no avail.

As it continued to grow, it finally reached the point where it was affecting the way I walked. Due to pain messages reaching the spinal reflex arc, I was as helpless to stop this as to prevent the knee jerk reflex that occurs when the right spot is hit with a hammer. So, by the following summer I had decided that I had better have it surgically removed, since my visualizations and my ministrations were not working, and I could not afford to risk my knee.

At the swimming pool one day, I was telling Rusty Kellogg, a physician friend visiting from New York, that I was unable to eliminate the corn on my foot and would probably have to have it surgically removed. Rusty asked to see it and said, "That's not a corn, it's a plantar wart." I had heard vaguely of such a thing, although I thought it was called a "planter's wart," and was something that farmers got if they walked barefoot in their fields.

Rusty explained that a plantar wart is caused by a virus, is highly vascularized, and is shaped something like an upside-down octopus, sending long tentacles up along the blood vessels. He said that they are very difficult to remove surgically and are hard to treat. I am sure he thought he was giving me bad news, but since I had been doing this work for some time and had seen what Garrett and others have been able to do, I thought, "Virus, vascularized— *good*, then I can get it with my white cells."

I was somewhat astonished myself with the rapidity of the results. In less than a week, it began to deteriorate and come apart. I discovered that at the outer end, this wart is built like a thick cable of packed wires, and now some of the fibers were coming loose and beginning to extrude.

I made the mistake of pulling on one of these. It was about three inches long and came out slowly, seeming to rip away from other tissues all the way. It hurt, but I couldn't stop because I didn't feel I wanted to cut if off, and also I didn't want to just leave it there. When it finally all came out, it bled quite a bit for a little while. Within two weeks the wart was completely gone, and it has never come back.

There are mysteries here that are not yet answered. During the entire time that this plantar wart was growing,

I had an excellent immune system. I did not have a single episode of cold or flu. Why did my immune system ignore the wart during all that time? And why did it attack the wart as soon as I directed its attention to it?

Warts have interested many physicians. Lewis Thomas, president of the Memorial Sloan-Kettering Cancer Center, has written a whole chapter on warts and their mysterious behavior in his book, *The Medusa and the Snail.* He notes that warts, the elaborate reproductive apparatus of a virus, can be removed by "something that can only be called thinking, or something like thinking. This is a special property of warts which is absolutely astonishing, more of a surprise than cloning or recombinant DNA or endorphin or acupuncture or anything else currently attracting attention in the press." This process may seem astonishing and certainly is of that magnitude of importance, but surely the attribution must be made that it is a special property of *thinking* that has caused the warts to go away, not a special property of warts.

Physicians often believe that visualization cannot work since the visualizer would have to know all the immune responses. Which lymphocytes in which combinations of killer cells and supressor cells, B cells and T cells, would be needed? How could the unconscious figure out all the mechanisms needed? Very frequently, patients also initially believe that they need to understand exactly *how* to direct their immune system in order to do it successfully.

The unconscious is a master at figuring out all sorts of complex relationships and mechanisms, as can be attested by its rapid generation of the myriad physiologic responses throughout all the systems of the body that we call the "flight or fight" response when it perceives threat. The very same physiologic responses are generated by the unconscious at *imagined* threat; the lower brain centers cannot tell the difference between a perception and an image but only respond to the amount of affect connected to either.

Andrew Weil also has devoted an entire chapter to warts in his book *Holistic Health*. He describes dramatic cures of warts in response to all sorts of treatments, none of which has anything in common except a belief that they will work. Weil states:

> *It is revealing of the limitations of materialistic science that no serious research exists on wart cures in response to treatments based on belief. I can think of few medical phenomena more deserving of study. When a wart that has persisted for months or years falls off within hours of being rubbed by a cut potato, the cure may look miraculous, but it is not mystical. Some analyzable, physical mechanism must underlie the event, one that uses familiar body components such as nerves and blood [and lymphocytes]. It would be valuable to identify and understand that mechanism, because it is so powerful, precise, and efficient, . . . Think of the possibility of directing that mechanism against malignant tumors or obstructions in coronary arteries or calcium deposits in joints! The prevalence of wart cures argues that the mechanism exists in everyone. Clearly, the switch that turns it on is located in the mind!*

And finally, before leaving the subject of warts entirely, there is this: a memo received in February 1974 from a colleague.

I thought you and your colleagues would want to hear the true story of my next door neighbor ... and his warts, as related to me by his mother ... Last summer, five-year-old M went to his family doctor for some minor surgery. Once the doctor had M anesthetized, he suggested to [his mother] that he remove the warts from his hand, warts that had caused a lot of embarrassment. She approved the idea, as did M its realization once he came to.

Well, a month or so later M was angry to find warts coming back at him. He and his mother consulted the doctor, who advised them to watch and wait.

Around this time, his mother read an article about imagery and healing and told M about the Porter boy's [Garrett's] success against his brain tumor. M listened closely, and decided that he too would imagine his body as having Pac Men at its disposal—to send in to gobble up the warts.

Off and on during the next three weeks, his mother would catch him staring into space abstractedly. When she asked him what he was doing, he would say he was thinking about his Pac Men. At the end of the three weeks, the warts were gone—never to return (at least not so far). "I thunk them away" is the way M accounted for their departure.

Constancy: Another Key to Successful Visualization

A partial explanation for the rapidity of this response brings me to the next condition for effective visualization, and that is *constancy*. In getting rid of my own wart, I started by visualizing white cells streaming down my leg, attacking and vanquishing all the wart cells and viruses. Because my foot was hurting quite a bit when I walked on it, I developed a "quickie" visualization of "hurt—squirt! hurt—squirt! hurt—squirt!," seeing white cells rushing down to the wart with every step. This is also a very beneficial way to utilize pain.

Jack Schwartz is a western yogi from Holland who now teaches and counsels in the United States. He has described pain as one of the best friends of the body, a friend who must be recognized and respected as such. It prevents us from sitting on a hot radiator, or continuing to hold something hot in our hand; it also prevents us from ignoring some interior condition that needs attention. In other words, it is an alarm that warns us to take action. Like the alarm clock that awakens us in the morning, we are grateful to it for the reminder, but need not let it ring all day. Once we have taken notice, we shut off the alarm.

Of course, there are some relentless and unremitting pains that are not easily shut off, but a good portion of almost any pain is fear, tension and resistance to feeling our feelings. The more we tense against and resist pain, the more it clamors for recognition. We get caught up in a vicious circle.

There are many excellent techniques for working with pain including holding, literally or in consciousness, the affected part, feeling it, caring for it, "melting into" the pain, expanding it (like a gas, so that it becomes more and more tenuous), transforming it to another sensation like warmth or tingling, and so on.

The bottom line, or most significant useful way of dealing with pain in cancer or other disease processes, is to first respect it for its function. I encourage patients who are doing visualization to greet the pain with a thought like, "Thank you, body, for reminding me to do my visualization again." As described, the visualization includes bringing blood flow into the area, breathing deeply and imagining breathing right into the area of pain, along with visualization of the immune system attacking the cancer.

Fear and anxiety can be handled in the same way. Cancer patients very frequently fear every discomfort and pain as a possible sign that there is new cancer growing. This technique of thanking the body for its request for help and then sending blood flow, vigilant white cells, and all the body's natural healing resources to the area, is helpful in decreasing these fears, too. It is the *opposite* of denial. If the pain persists, the patient is encouraged to follow up with a call to their physician or to ask about it in the next office visit. This helps to mitigate against new symptoms being repressed or denied out of fear.

I also encourage patients to employ a sort of "constant instant practice" as we do in instructing people in the acquisition of any self-regulation skill. Every time you come to a stop sign, every time you pick up or hang up the phone, and whenever your mind can think of it, visualize your immune system doing its job, kinesthetically, inside the body. This can be done briefly and in the same way as kinesthetically visualizing yourself serving a tennis ball, or touching your toes, or any other familiar activity. With the mind'e eye, *see* what you want to have happen happening; *feel* it happening inside your body.

One further device was to elicit the continuing support of Garrett's "unconscious" in combating the tumor when he was not actively doing his visualization. I explained to him on several occasions that just as his blood continued to circulate, his heart to beat, and his digestion to go on with-

112

out his conscious intervention, so could his immune system continue to battle his tumor, with the while cells continuing to stream to his tumor site even when he wasn't thinking about it and wasn't doing the visualization. During therapy sessions we often did the visualization together as a dialogue. At these times, he gave much free play to his imagery, and we were able to handle unconscious messages as they emerged.

Intention: A Blueprint for Successful Visualization

It is important to see your goal met, the tumor or cancer cells destroyed, and the healing accomplished, every time you do the visualization. This represents your *intention* and provides a *blueprint* for your body to follow. Just as a blueprint for a house is real even before the foundation is dug, so this blueprint is a real description of the plan for the body, even though it takes some time for the body to heal. It may be that an image of the present condition will pop back into your mental picture as soon as this visualization is completed. That is perfectly natural; simply see the process through to completion the next time you do the visualization.

Garrett practiced one or another of his visualizations at least once daily. During these visualizations, he was encouraged to continue the sequence until he saw the tumor as completely destroyed. He understood the visualization was like a blueprint. Although the tumor would not be completely destroyed in one session, it established the intent just as an architect's blueprint establishes the intent of the kind of house that is to be built. The blueprint is true, as an intention, even before the foundation is laid. In the same way, he visualized both the process and the final outcome desired each time he did his visualization.

When medical treatment such as chemotherapy and radiation is being given, visualizing it as being powerful and effective is of the utmost importance. Patients often have an ambivalent attitude—almost a love-hate relationship—with their treatment. The unconscious dichotomous attitude is "I must have this to live" and "This is killing me."

The way in which people visualize their treatment, as well as the images, conscious and unconscious, that they have of the treatment, is a major factor in how their bodies will respond to the treatment. Uncovering unconscious attitudes of fear and distrust of the treatment, and dealing with them, is essential. We are *always* imaging what we are doing and going to do, and visualizing outcomes, so it is not a question of IF we will image but only of *what* and *how,* and of making it a part of conscious self-regulation rather than something that is happening willy-nilly, for better or for worse.

The Importance of a Positive Attitude

A positive attitude toward treatment, feeling it as a true helper to the body's well-being, even if temporarily it is very tough, is very important. To patients, I have likened the treatment to inviting a police SWAT team or a national guard crack team into the neighborhood to help put down trouble. They don't come to stay, but their help when needed is indispensable. The treatments are the most powerful agents that medical science has to offer against their particular type of cancer. Although the treatments may be tough on the whole system, the healthy cells are strong and resilient and can resist harm and repair themselves, whereas the cancer cells are weak and confused and cannot survive.

It is very helpful to use a positive visualization of the treatment and its outcome while receiving it. Good suggestions for this include emotional preparation beforehand, perhaps bringing favorite music to the treatment and playing it during the treatment. During the treatment itself, welcome the radiation or the chemicals into the body as a powerful helper. Again, the best visualizations are those that patients develop themselves, but I have found that in general patients need more help with this, probably because the treatment is not an internal process and therefore is not "known" to the unconscious parts of the brain.

Develop Specific Visualizations for Specific Uses

For radiation treatments, a good suggestion is to visualize the rays coming into the body like shining bursts of energy that demolish the weak cancer cells; all the healthy cells can be seen as mirrors, resisting damage and reflecting the radiation directly onto the tumor. For chemotherapy, golden bullets that are directed against the cancer cells, surging into the blood stream, make a good image. The treatment is an important ally to the white cells, and their partnership can be visualized.

It is interesting that the best imagery for the immune system consists of powerful beings of some sort, whether human or animal, that possess conscious intentionality and are responsive to direction. The Simontons, Achterberg and Lawlis, and I have found that inanimate imagery such as giant hoses or vacuum cleaners is not as powerful. However, I have not encountered imagery of the treatment being represented as living beings, in spite of my comparing the treatment to a police SWAT team in a neighborhood, either in the literature or in my patients. One can speculate quite reasonably that this is because the white cells are alive and responsive, and the treatment is not.

Visualizing the chemotherapy as potent and working *with* it in the body potentiates its action, adding all the biological effects of belief and expectation to its other effects. This also helps decrease the adverse side effects that arise from resistance to the medication. Imagery and visualization of the chemotherapy also increase inner awareness of the drug/body interaction and of the build-up of chemical action in the body.

One patient who was an excellent visualizer illustrates this point. Leonard embarked on a total holistic health program when he was diagnosed with Stage IIB Hodgkins Disease. This approach fit very well with his interests and values. After a trip to M.D. Anderson Hospital for a second opinion, he opted for chemotherapy and psychophysiological therapy and began both treatments at the same time. He began a whole health routine which included yoga and other regular exercise for approximately an hour every morning, high nutrition, and meditation as well.

He was a good visualizer and became very sensitive to receiving messages from his unconscious body/mind. He visualized his immune system and his chemotherapy working together in partnership. He did very well with this combination and very well with his chemotherapy. Then at one point after several months of chemotherapy treatment, he began to feel that his body was saturated with the chemotherapy drugs, and the balance between it and his immune system was not being maintained. He decided to stop chemotherapy for the time being, not because he didn't want its aid in his system, but because he could tell he had more than enough of it in his system.

Leonard continued to visit his oncologist, who wished he would continue the treatments but was willing to be supportive of his decision to stop chemotherapy. Now, a year and one-half later, he is still in remission. Leonard and his oncologist have continued to work together as a team to keep him well, and he has taken responsibility for his own body through having regular check-ups and following his health program faithfully.

At times, with small children and also with older children and adults who are very concrete in their thinking, it is possible to use props on which people can focus their visualization. A beautiful example of this comes from the work of Leslie Salov, an opthalmologist and founder of the Vision and Health Center in Whitewater, Wisconsin. Sara was four and one-half years old when Dr. Salov worked with her. She had five blood angiomas behind her left eyeball, and attempts at conventional medical treatment had proved unsuccessful. It was decided that the best course of action would be to wait until the eye was pushed out of its socket, then to clean out and heal the orbit, and provide her with a glass eye. When Dr. Salov first saw her, Sara's eye was protruding by three-quarters of a centimeter.

After explaining clearly in her terms what was happening to her eye, he asked her to draw it, and she made a picture of her face, the five tumors, and a heart, on which she had inscribed "love, Sara." He next told her that each day her mother would give her a syringe filled with red colored water and a pail, and he instructed her to squeeze the red water out of the syringe while looking at her picture and imaging her tumors getting smaller just as the syringe was doing. When he asked her to explain the process back to him, her description included the phrase that she would see herself squeezing out the liquid and see the syringe getting smaller "just like those bags of blood behind my eyes are going to do." Her use of this phrase made him sure she understood what to do.

The rest of the treatment consisted of nutritional changes and the use of color, as he instructed her parents to surround her with the color blue. In less than two months, her eye was restored to its normal position, and the tumors were gone.

"Well, I don't get angry, okay? I mean I have a tendency to internalize. I can't express anger. That's one of the problems I have. I—I grow a tumor instead."

—ISAAC DAVIS IN "MANHATTAN"
BY WOODY ALLEN AND MARSHALL BRICKMAN

A cheerful heart is a good medicine, but a downcast spirit dries up the bones.

—PROVERBS 17:22

The greatest discovery of my generation is that human beings, by changing the inner attitudes of their minds, can change the outer aspect of their lives. It is too bad that more people will not accept this tremendous discovery and begin living with it.

—WILLIAM JAMES

CHAPTER FIVE

Beliefs, Attitudes, and Expectations

The Relationship between Personality and Cancer

*I*s there such a thing as a *cancer personality?* Is there a cluster of cancer personalities for different types of cancer? The evidence, though vast and multidimensional, is not yet considered to be conclusive.

For nearly two thousand years, since Galen's observation in the second century that cancer accompanied melancholic personalities, observers have likened personality, or aspects of personality, to malignancy. The difficulty, in terms of the kind of hard scientific proof that is considered desirable, is the fact that most of these observations are ex post facto. Until very recently, few prospective studies have been done. Those that do exist, as well as all the many retrospective studies and observations, confirm a predisposing set of personality factors, attitudes, and beliefs.

Steven Locke and Mady Hornig-Rohan have edited a recent comprehensive annotated bibliography linking immune competence with the mind. *Mind and Immunity: Behavioral Immunology* contains 1304 articles and nearly 150 books, book chapters, and review articles dealing with the relationship of mind and immunity. In it, forty-nine papers on the topic of Personality and Cancer are cited. Most of these support a relationship between cancer and personality factors, with the predominant factor being depression and the helplessness/hopelessness syndrome. In many studies significant loss, in childhood or shortly predating the onset of illness or both, was also found.

One of the most interesting, and conclusive, evidences of the effect of personality on physiology comes from recent studies of people with multiple personalities. People with multiple personalities, like those made well known in books and movies such as *The Three Faces of Eve* and *Sybil,* have always created interest because of their strange switches in behavioral characteristics. The changes in behavior have included different body language, sometimes accents, speech mannerisms, handwriting, hobbies and skills, and different phobias and memories.

New interest is being generated by the fact that these people not only change behavior, but their brains and their bodies also change. Different personalities within one person have different brain wave patterns, different handedness, and different allergies. Eyeglass prescriptions and such objective measures as eye pressure and corneal curvature differ. A person may be nearsighted or farsighted in different personalities or even be colorblind in one but not another. As they change from personality to personality, these people experience dramatic physical characteristic changes as well.

Bennett Braun, a Chicago psychiatrist who has studied a number of persons with multiple personality disorder, notes that these changes in physiology are not greater than those that can be achieved through hypnosis. And this implies, in turn, at least theoretically, that there are no changes achieved through hypnosis that could not also be achieved through voluntary control. After all, the hypnotist holds no strings within the body of his subject. The person with multiple personality is controlling all the changes in physiology made, albeit unconsciously. Conscious control of the unconscious can be learned, perhaps of any system over time and surely over any system that can be affected by personality shifts or by hypnosis.

Early in their work connected with the psychological management of malignancy, Carl and Stephanie Simonton compiled an annotated bibliography. They reviewed the medical literature concerned with the etiology of cancer, and in more than two hundred articles they found a relationship between personality factors, emotional factors, and cancer. They found the most prevalent predisposing condition to be the loss of an important love object or relationship six to eighteen months prior to the diagnosis of malignancy. According to the authors, these losses create hopelessness because they recapitulate lack of closeness, loss, or rejection experienced in childhood. The most common personality characteristics they found were a tendency to hold resentments, difficulty in forgiving others, a tendency toward self-pity, poor ability to develop and maintain long-term relationships, a poor self-image, and feelings of rejection in general.

Claus Bahnson, in his overviews, "Stress and Cancer: The State of the Art," Parts 1 and 2, finds recurring themes of loneliness and hopelessness stemming from lack of a loving, protected childhood. Personality characteristics of inhibition, rigidity, repression and denial, when combined with the stress of loss and depression, seem to increase vulnerability to clinical cancer.

Lawrence LeShan, during the first five years of his research into personality and cancer, tested and interviewed over 450 patients and found that 72% of them had particular life-history events and personality characteristics that occurred in only 10% of a non-cancer control group. As he explored their case histories, he determined that these personality characteristics preceded the onset of cancer by many years and generally developed in childhood, when the patients often felt rejected and unloved and were constantly searching for ways to please others, inhibiting expression of their own feelings of anger and hostility in order to gain acceptance. They were generally thought by others to be fine, gentle, and uncomplaining people.

In discussing *how* personality might affect the genesis of cancer, there are two major theories. By far the most prevalent is the theory that the immunologic defenses are weakened, and hormonal and endocrine balances are upset by the biochemical changes that accompany depression, repressed hostility, and feelings of helplessness. If immunologic defenses are weakened, this leads to a sort of "double whammy." The body is more vulnerable to the various carcinogens present in the environment, and it is more likely to produce cancerous cells. Also, cancer cells, once present, have a greater chance to multiply unchallenged.

The other theory, born out in part by observations and research on types of cancer related to specific experiences or personality configurations, is that psychic energy from frustrated desires or subjective losses can appear somatically as an attempt on the part of the unconscious—the lower brain centers—to replace the lost object or object of desire biologically. In the latter, the type and location of the tumor symbolically match the psychological experience of loss.

In either case, stress can deter the elimination of tumor and cancer cells by impairing immune surveillance. Stress can facilitate an increase in the growth of tumors by neuroendocrine changes, mediated by the autonomic nervous system through the limbic-hypothalamic-pituitary axis. Corticosteroids associated with stress inhibit lymphocyte proliferation and metabolism.

In "A Biopsychosocial Approach to Immune Function and Medical Disorders," Marvin Stein suggests that as evidence is accumulating and knowledge unfolding of the various ways that psychosocial factors are related to immune functions, predisposing risk factors are being discovered which can provide a means for studying individuals prior to the onset of disease.

The common underlying factor in personality and stress seems to be a lack of coping ability in some way. Studies linking cancer and personality, and cancer and stress, are increasing all the time. In spite of this, there is no absolute evidence that stress causes cancer—but that it is a predisposing risk factor, there can be no doubt. However, cancer is not just one, but more than a hundred diseases. Factors influencing cancer and predisposing to cancer include genetics, diet and nutritional status, carcinogens present in the environment, radiation and excess sunlight, as well as factors stemming from mind and behavior. But regardless of whether or not stress causes cancer, there is general agreement that the body's ability to fight cancer is hindered by stress and that the body's immune defenses are compromised by stress.

For a cancer patient, there is a triple stress to deal with. There is the stress which predated the cancer and which seems always to have been present prior to diagnosis. There is the stress of having cancer and dealing with the threat to self-identify and personal security. And there is the stress of a treatment that can be uncomfortable, frightening, and depleting.

Learning to Choose Our Responses

Fortunately, humans are learners. We can change how we perceive stress and how our bodies respond to the stressors in our lives. We can acquire the skills and resources for dealing with stress as a challenge and as a learning opportunity. Learning self-regulation of responses to stress gradually leads the learner to meet change with a sense of energy and exhilaration rather than worry and despair, and this can have a powerful healing effect.

The idea that we can assume responsibility for the course of our illness suggests to some people that patients are being accused of causing their cancer, that guilt might be aroused by such an idea. Of course no one chooses to have cancer or causes their body to become cancerous in any conscious way. But the way our bodies unconsciously respond to stress may be, and probably is, a contributing factor in every stress-related illness. This is *good* news. It means there is something we can do to affect it in a positive manner.

There are other studies which look at the characteristics of survivors of cancer. There are also personal characteristics which increase the chance of survival, and these can be actively acquired.

The Simontons, together with Jeanne Achterberg, made a study of survivors, examining the characteristics of their own patients who outlived predicted life expectancies. All of the patients who choose their program are screened on the basis of a stated willingness to cooperate with their medical treatment and assume a responsibility for their own return to health. The exceptional patients refuse to give up, rate higher than average in nonconformity and ego strength, and have an inner-directed locus of control.

Kenneth Pelletier cited four significant factors present in those who survived cancer against the odds. Each of the patients had gone through some profound intrapsychic changes; their sense of self and innermost being had been changed, whether by a revelatory experience, meditation and prayer, or spiritual insight. They made important interpersonal changes, improving their relations with others. All had made major changes in their diet and nutrition and in the ways they cared for their bodies. And every one, without exception, looked upon their recovery not as a gift or a miracle, and not as a spontaneous remission, but as a long, hard struggle that they had won!

While a doctoral student at Harvard, Erik Peper compiled a list of so-called spontaneous remissions from cancer. A computer search of the medical literature from the Library of Congress and the medical libraries at Harvard and MIT yielded about four hundred articles which comprised his annotated bibliography. The circumstances surrounding the remissions were as varied as can be imagined; people used all their favorite methods, from religious sojourns to nutritional approaches, fasts, and lifestyle changes. The common ground among all these cases of remission lies in the assumption of self-regulation, the assumption of responsibility in some way, and a change of attitude involving hope, personal effort, determination, and other positive feelings.

Placebo or Visualization? The Case for Positive Thinking

The effect of belief and expectation has never been more clearly or dramatically illustrated than in the case of the man with cancer who believed in Krebiozen. This case is very famous in certain medical circles and is worth mentioning.

This is a true story about a man who had advanced cancer (lymphosarcoma) and was lingering very near death. Every possible medical treatment had been tried. His body was filled with huge tumor masses, the size of oranges, and his liver and spleen were enormous. He required oxygen most of the time, and every other day one or two quarts of fluid had to be removed from his chest because his thoracic duct was obstructed. He was in a terminal state, but he was filled with hope even though his doctors were not.

The reason this man was so filled with hope was that he had been waiting for medical science to discover a cure, and now he believed that this was accomplished. He had read about Krebiozen, and now he knew that the hospital where he lay dying had been chosen to test it. He wasn't really eligible to be included in the research, since one of the requirements was that patients on whom Krebiozen was tried must have a life expectancy of at least three, and preferably six, months. But he was so enthusiastic and begged his physician for what he called a "golden opportunity," that the physician felt he had to include him.

The first injection of Krebiozen was given to him on a Friday, and on the following Monday, the physician thought that his patient might be dead, and his supply of Krebiozen could be transferred to someone else. When the patient had received the injection, he was completely bed-ridden, gasping for air. On this Monday morning, he was walking around the ward, happily showing everyone he could find how wonderfully well he was doing with this new miracle drug. The tumor masses had "melted like snow-balls on a stove" and were less than half their size already. His physicians said that this was a more dramatic change than could be expected from radiation treatment given each of these three days. Very excited, the doctor rushed to see the other patients who had received Krebiozen injec-tions, but none of them had changed. Very soon, the man was recovered completely, left the hospital, and even re-sumed flying his airplane with no discomfort, even though only a few short weeks before he had been gasping in an oxygen mask.

He continued to do just fine until controversy about the drug's usefulness began to appear in the papers, as clinic after clinic was finding no results. He began to lose faith in his last hope, and in spite of two months of practi-cally perfect health, he became gloomy and miserable. At this point his tumors came back with full force, and he again appeared before his physician in almost the same ter-minal condition.

As if this was not amazing enough, the second chapter of this story is even more amazing. His physician, seizing upon a golden opportunity of his own, told this patient that it had just been discovered that the reason Krebiozen had been failing to achieve its initial promise was that it had a very short shelf life, quickly losing potency. He said that now there was available some Krebiozen that was very new and potent and that a shipment was expected in the next day or two. The man's faith was restored, and he was very excited and hopeful. A couple of days later, when his expectancy was very high, the doctor administered an injection of sterile water. The man's recovery was even more dramatic than the first time. His tumors melted, his chest fluid vanished, and he went back to flying once more. As long as the water injections continued, he remained symptom-free. When the final judgment of Krebiozen by the American Medical Association appeared in the press, finding the drug worthless in treating cancer, he was readmitted to the hospital and soon died.

How are we to understand this? Did the man have two "spontaneous remissions"? This case clearly demonstrates the wondrous power of the mind when, bolstered by faith and expectation, it visualizes an outcome. That is exactly what the placebo *effect* is—the effect of a visualization, one that is thoroughly believed in. Isn't this what we should be trying to engender in all patients and in ourselves as well?

The placebo effect as a visualization was discussed by Elmer Green in his Presidential Address to the Biofeedback Society of America titled, "Psychophysiologic Correlates of Expectancy." In the paper, he brought together converging information from ethology, psychodynamic theory, autogenic training theory, the psychology of perception, and neuroanatomy and the neuropysiologic correlates of sensory discrimination. Speaking of the placebo effect, he said,

> *It is now clear, at least to me, that what is called the placebo effect is a subdivision of the self-regulation effect.*

> *Humans, through visualization, are able to self-trigger physiological behaviors that in animals are associated, as far as we know, only with external perceptions of some kind. It is this fact in humans,*

*of course, which gives rise to the placebo effect. The
placebo, by definition, is something false by means of
which a patient is tricked into using his or her own
visualization powers for physiological manipulation.
Not everyone has yet thought of it this way, I know,
but if a placebo is put into a cup of coffee with
instruction to a patient, "Drink this and it will slow
your heart rate," it can happen. If the same sugar
pill is slipped into the coffee* **unknown** *to the patient,
however, nothing happens. This is because the
visualization and the expectancy associated with
that visualization are not triggered off.*

*As a species, we have probably been using this
general effect since we differentiated from the
animals, but now,* **for the first time in the history of
humanity, it has become possible to get the
information from inside the skin.** *Information before
biofeedback was normally fed back only to
subcortical brain centers for unconscious autonomic
and homeostatic regulation. Now, for the first time in
human history, this information is coming back to
the* **cortex,** *and because we can visualize changes in
the body, biofeedback is making it quite easy to
regulate many heretofore involuntary processes.*

The Vital Role of Biofeedback in Self-Regulation

In the *Cancer Journal for Clinicians,* Norman Cousins
wrote a guest editorial titled, "Cancer and Placebos." Because of his own experiences in self-healing, Cousins was

appointed Adjunct Professor in the Department of Psychiatry and Behavioral Medicine in the U.C.L.A. School of Medicine. In the editorial, he examines the role of mind in healing and the relationship between mind and medicine in every way.

Cousins noted that recently the placebo is being studied in terms of its ability to change human chemistry. A bibliography of placebo research by three of his colleagues in the Neuropsychiatric Institute at U.C.L.A. listed 674 studies, many of which showed that people who respond to placebos release secretions in their brains that in turn produce specific physiological effects in their bodies. What Norman Cousins wanted to share with doctors was this: if a placebo is an emotional experience that can trigger a biochemical response, there is an important therapeutic value in a patient's belief in the healing power of the physician. *What* a physician communicates to a patient and *how* he communicates it can have a powerful impact on the treatment outcome.

Perhaps every illness we ever have is in response to a problem of some type and is an attempt at a solution. A life-threatening illness like cancer may be a response to loss and despair, or it may be an unconscious attempt to replace something or to escape from some perceived or imagined inadequacy. Human reactions to stress and loss can cause cancer. This should not be interpreted as saying, "I caused this cancer"; however, the illness can act like an *attention getter*. Something internal needs to be dealt with.

Faced with a diagnosis of cancer, patients react in a number of different ways. Many patients would like to get well but want the doctor to invest all the energy and effort, seeing themselves as passive recipients of treatment. To a large extent, our culture fosters this. We are taught to believe that everything—or almost everything—can be resolved by popping a pill or by having something taken out. In fact, there is a tendency to be insulted and outraged when we discover that there is no easy cure for something that we have. Often physicians encourage us to take a passive role, follow instructions, and be compliant. In fact, patient compliance is a very large issue in both psychiatric and physical medicine. So the patient may expect to be cured, or hope to be cured, but wants the doctor to take all the responsibility. Physicians often don't know how, or are afraid, to tap patient potential for self-healing and encourage patient participation in the healing process.

A much smaller percentage of people seem quite ready to give up the moment the diagnosis is delivered, if not before. Once they discover they have cancer, it becomes the central focus of their lives. All their plans are organized around having cancer, and consciously or unconsciously they think of themselves almost as though they were already in the grave. Their self-image is that they are dying, and as if following a script they act out this role to the finish.

Another group of patients is willing to do anything to get well. No effort seems too great. This is a characteristic shared by survivors of catastrophic and life-threatening illness. Most importantly, it is an attitude that can be acquired. One thing that survivors have in common is a practice of envisioning themselves getting well.

A young man who experienced this type of change in a dramatic way told of his experience to a national audience on the television program "Good Morning America." He was a graduate student at Harvard when he was diagnosed as having cancer and began treatment with chemotherapy. After a few months, he felt he could no longer go on with the treatments. He felt tired, weak, and depressed, and he told his physician he was withdrawing from chemotherapy. His doctor told him he would be signing his own death warrant, and he said he did not care. He went home and, feeling entirely frustrated and angry, put on a pair of running shorts and went for a run. Then he exercised, swam, and finally returned home, exhausted but happier than he had been for some time. He became aware that he felt better for the first time in a long time and decided it was because he had taken charge of his life. During the ensuing months, he took up rowing, boxing, running, racqetball, and swimming, and he filled his life with taking care of his body and building strength. When he felt strong and positive and wanting to live, when he could envision himself getting well, he returned to chemotherapy and this time completed it with very little difficulty, maintaining his active life. That was more than six years ago, and he has been free of cancer ever since.

As beliefs and expectations have biological consequences, so do attitudes. There are definite neuroendocrine and neurohormone accompaniments to a good mood, to a strong positive attitude.

Lisa is one of the people who illustrates this power of attitude. She is one of the most lively, fun and laughter-loving, vivacious people I know. She is also a person with strong values and beliefs, and her life and her profession give her ample opportunity to put them into practice. She has defied all the odds and is considered by some to be a medical miracle.

In the fall of 1972, just after she turned seventeen, Lisa was diagnosed as having acute myeloblastic or myelocytic leukemia. Her older brother had been killed in an automobile accident sixteen months earlier, and the stresses and pain in her family had been considerable ever since. Her parents were told that she had only three weeks to live, but she was treated with chemotherapy and gained a long remission. When she began to recover, they were told that the first relapse would mean an automatic death sentence, but she was not told this. She entered college in Des Moines and made arrangements to continue her chemotherapy treatments there. She was told by a physician there, when she had been in remission for over four years, that she was almost to the point of five year's remission, which was a good thing since if she had a relapse, she could not live through it. At the time, she believed this pronouncement totally.

In the fall of 1978, she had that first relapse. She was in the second year of law school. She had had a close group of friends as an undergraduate, everything had gone well for her, and she began to think of herself as invulnerable. When she went to law school, she left these friends behind and got into a round of very hard work. As she became somewhat tired and lonely, she began to think the cancer could come back. She came down with a fever and sore throat, and she knew immediately what it was. She went back and started chemotherapy all over again and achieved a substantial remission for about nine months. In her words, this was the first medically impossible thing that happened. At the time, she remembered that she had been told she could not survive a relapse, but once she *had* relapsed, she didn't believe it and felt inside that she did not have to accept that outcome.

Many professional therapists and physicians feel that such a strong will to live represents denial. It appears that if the person does not conform to the conventional and expected idea of the course of their illness, then they are suffering from denial—denial of *what?* Steven Appelbaum, in discussing the topic of denial and the failure to adequately study the psychological effects on cancer, has this to say:

> ... *the options are few and clear. One can assume that one has a hopeless disease, that one's chances for survival are dictated irrevocably by the statistics attached to one's disease and its treatment. Or one can embrace the assumption that control can be asserted over the disease, that its development and maintenance can be understood according to psychological dimensions, and that if one works at it one may create a new set of statistics. It is a choice that the therapist, as well as the patient, has to make.*

Six months after her husband of only four days was killed in an automobile accident, Lisa had another relapse. Her subsequent medical history has been a continuous round of full and partial remissions and relapses. Her physicians are continuously amazed that she continues to rebound.

Lisa has the office across the hall from mine, where she is an attorney for Legal Services for Prisoners. When I first knew her, she did not tell anyone that she had leukemia. As she puts it, other people's reactions are often less than helpful. However, she had the Simontons' book, *Getting Well Again,* and was doing visualization and following their guidelines on her own.

Because she has not encountered all the other illnesses that generally accompany acute leukemia of her type, the original diagnosis is now being questioned. Nevertheless, she has had a number of complications, one of which was a myeloblastoma on her leg.

This myeloblastoma, a tumor made of live leukemic cells, was growing and was occasionally painful. Worse, it compromised her circulation and was a cause of great concern. A number of X-rays were taken of it, and it was also biopsied. Her physicians were contemplating amputation of her leg, since there was no other treatment considered feasible. Lisa began working on the tumor with visualization, and she and I also did a visualization session. Once she began visualizing her white cells attacking it and eliminating it totally, as a blueprint signaling her intentions to her body, it disappeared in a very short time. It remains absent to this date, more than a year later. Interestingly, in spite of the biopsy and all the X-rays, her physicians now deny that this tumor was ever there. It simply does not fit their belief system of what can happen.

Lisa is in remission again and happily married. Her energy, her strong positivity in every aspect of her life, and her unique blend of compassion and humor unleash a life force and energy that sustain her through everything. Her story represents a constancy of healing.

It was certainly in recognition of the role of attitude in healing that caused Jerry Jampolsky to choose the name, "The Center for Attitudinal Healing." The center is founded on the idea that the most powerful healing force in the world is love. As Jerry said on the award-winning film, *Donahue and Kids,* "We believe the mind *does* control the body, and we *do* have a will to live; what we have done is give the added ingredient of *love.* The love and unity is the healing experience."

The psychological effect of cancer or other life-threatening and catastrophic illness on people can go one of two ways. Either they identify themselves as very sick, dying, and that becomes the organizing principle of their lives, or they begin to experience every moment as precious and to reconstruct their priorities and become more open in their relationships, more consciously aware of love and warmth that they previously took for granted.

The children in the center help teach each other that they can choose one thought over another, they can choose peace instead of worry, love instead of fear. In *Donahue and Kids,* a number of the children state that the experience of having cancer contributed something very important to them. They have learned that in helping each other, they help themselves. They have learned that they can experience one day at a time and not live in regret over the past or worry about the future. They have learned that they have the power of choice. In combating their illness, these children have learned the greatest lessons of life.

. . . But, on the whole, tho' I never arrived at the perfection I had been so ambitious of obtaining, but fell far short of it, yet I was, by the endeavor, a better and happier man than I otherwise should have been if I had not attempted it . . .

—BENJAMIN FRANKLIN

Our message . . . is the assertion of hope, of faith in every individual's potential for growth and development and self-transcendence. It is a declaration of love for and of belief in one's fellow creatures.

—KARL MENNINGER

CHAPTER SIX

The Road Toward Wellness

*W*e follow a wellness model with all our patients in the Biofeedback and Psychophysiology Center. This is especially important for cancer patients who often are in failing health or who think of themselves in that way. Our protocol is designed to help patients restore and/or maintain the greatest level of health possible. The rationale for this is that cancer will have less chance of taking over a healthy, optimally-functioning body. To this end, our approach takes into account, as much as possible, each aspect of the whole person: physical, emotional, cognitive, and spiritual.

It's easy, and it's hard. It's easy because of the body's pro-homeostatic tendencies, and it's easy because the mind-brain-body *already* knows exactly how to do it. The examples in this book demonstrate that our bodies can be directed to do many things, not the least of which is getting rid of warts and tumors. Countless examples from medical hypnosis abound which demonstrate that with suggestion, the body can carry out complex responses.

Swami Rama's statement that all of the body is in the mind but not all of the mind is in the body suggests the existence of a metaprogrammer, a center of consciousness, however we wish to conceive of our larger self, that can make choices which affect the brain/behavior/body continuum. Brain, behavior, and body are inseparable, and one cannot be affected to the slightest degree, or change in the slightest degree, without comparably affecting the other two. It is these two facts—the natural body wisdom and the psychophysiological principle—that make self-regulation of healing possible.

Components of Wellness

A *physically* healthy lifestyle requires exercise, good nutrition, good breathing and plenty of oxygen, and the capacity to relax deeply. An *emotionally* healthy lifestyle includes fun and enjoyment, some goals that can be met, good relations with others, and a will to live fully in the moment, which is the only time we have. *Mentally* good health is demonstrated in part by freedom of choice, by participation, by some creative or constructive or productive way of meeting problems that arise. *Spiritual* health is the core of our being, and we are most healthy when we are in touch with and informed by our spirit, in whatever way we understand that.

Exercise is an important part of the program, something we advocate and encourage. I think the exercise should be as vigorous and as much fun as is practical and possible. We help our patients to find exercise that is suitable to them, to their abilities and preferences. The exercises should improve flexibility, muscle tone, and general health. These exercises may include walking, running, and stretching, as well as more vigorous games like tennis and racquetball if the person is up to them. Yoga and Tai Chi are good, and even Karate or Aikido are excellent choices for engendering a feeling of forcefulness and power.

Physical exercise is important in a symbolic way, too. It gives a message to our bodies, a message that we are working on ourselves, getting stronger, moving toward health. It is important to give this message to ourselves, even if the exercise we can do is very limited. Even a bedridden patient can do breathing exercises, tense and relax various muscle groups, flex fingers and toes, and do some things to improve strength and circulation.

Breathe: The Essence of Healthful Living

Breathing is an essential topic and an exercise in and of itself. Whole books have been written about the healthful effects of breathing. I have come to feel that breathing is so important that if we had only one tool or technique to share which would maximally affect physical health, I would choose breathing. In my own work I always emphasize breathing techniques, and so I will give the main ideas or instructions here so that the reader can follow them if desired.

The goal of the breathing exercises is to establish deep, diaphragmatic breathing, extended in depth and duration and providing maximal oxygenation of the entire body. The results can reduce anxiety and pain, promote tissue healing, decrease nausea, insomnia, and other unpleasant symptoms, and increase available energy.

The first thing to consider is the mechanics of breathing. Many people, when anxious, breathe rapidly and shallowly into the upper chest, keeping the upper and lower abdomen "sucked in" and immobilized. The first thing to do is to establish proper breathing motion in the body. The part of the abdomen over the diaphragm and the lowest part of the rib cage should expand with each in-breath and contract with each out-breath. The easiest way to accomplish this, at least for the exercise, is to start by lying flat on your back on the bed or floor. Place your hand on your abdomen just under your ribs in front. As you exhale, push your hand toward your backbone, pulling downward with the muscles there. Exhale completely.

It is very important to exhale as completely as you can, getting all the old, "re-breathed" air out of your lungs so you can fill them completely with fresh, oxygenated air. If you wanted to fill a glass with fresh water, you wouldn't leave it half full of stale water. In order to fill your lungs with fresh air, it is necessary to get the stale, carbon dioxide-filled air out.

When you inhale, raise your abdomen toward the ceiling and when exhaling, pull it back toward the floor. It is helpful to visualize a column of air rising toward the ceiling as you fill it with air and then falling back toward the floor as you empty it. The upper part of your chest should remain relaxed and as motionless as possible.

When the proper motion is established, assuring that you are breathing with your diaphragm, the next step is to establish deep, but not forced, inhalations and exhalations at a constant rate of flow, with no breath holding at the top or bottom of the breathing cycle. Find the highest number you can count to while exhaling and while inhaling. Try to keep the rate even, that is, be exhaling or inhaling the same amount of air on the last number as on the first. For example, you may find that you can count to four while exhaling and four while inhaling, but to try to count to five would be a strain. If you are trying to prolong your breath too much, you will experience a "jerking" of the diaphragm, a signal that your breathing rate has dropped below your metabolic requirements. Practice the exercise two or three times a day, counting to four, and after a week or so you may find you can count to six with comfort. If six is too much, drop back to five. Practice for another week, and then lengthen the duration again.

The goal of this exercise is to extend the breathing cycle, in both depth and duration, until your breathing rate during relaxation is gradually reduced, over a period of weeks, to three to five times a minute. This simple exercise has proven to be of immense help to our patients, particularly those who are experiencing any obstructions to their breathing, and to those who characteristically reflect anxiety in rapid, shallow breathing.

It is well to remember that cancer cells do not metabolize well in an oxygen-rich environment. Healthy cells metabolize by oxygenation, and cancer cells metabolize by fermentation, which requires a low oxygen environment.

As you continue to practice, you will develop an awareness of other times when you gasp and hold your breath as a way of blocking feelings. You will also become more aware of rapid, shallow breathing at times of anxiety, pain, and daily life stress. As you increase this awareness, you can re-establish deep, relaxed breathing with very beneficial effects on body and mind. You can learn to exhale, let go of tension, and breathe slowly and deeply as an instant de-stressing technique.

One of the most useful techniques is to imagine breathing directly into a part of the body that you wish to relieve and heal or strengthen. Directing the breath to different parts of the body is one of the oldest and most potent healing techniques. Imagine that you are breathing through this chosen organ or body part, bringing in oxygen and energy and activation with the in-breath, and eliminating tension, pain, inflammation, or whatever is appropriate with each out-breath.

Nutrition: You Are What You Eat

It is also useful, and perhaps essential, to pay special attention to nutrition when an illness is present. To maximize your body's resources to fight illness and restore itself, it seems wise to eliminate all foods that might interfere with this process and to eat in abundance the foods that promote energy and growth. We recommend avoidance of all "junk foods," sugar, as much as possible, white flour, and processed foods in general, at least for the duration. An abundance of fresh fruits and vegetables and whole grains and cereals is ideal. Eliminating fats is important, along with severely limiting red meat and all fried foods. Eating only moderate amounts of fish and poultry is ideal.

This is generally in conformance with the American Cancer Society's recommendations for a cancer-prevention diet, only more so. What better time to prevent the further growth of cancer than at a time when one already has some? Also, it would be wise to consult your physician or a nutritional expert about extra vitamins and minerals during this time. Some experts who provide diets are Max Gerson, Harold Manners, William Kelley, Nathan Pritikin, and Emanuel Cheraskin. All of them advocate similar diets and increased vitamin intake, and all consider Vitamin C to be especially important.

Doing all these healthy things for your body will give your whole self the message, consciously and unconsciously, that you are intending on getting better and are already in the process of doing so.

A patient of mine with lymphoma had become extremely weak with multiple infections, a severe case of shingles, and serious weight loss. She had been hospitalized and forced to discontinue all anti-cancer chemotherapy because of these conditions and a severely depleted immune system. She decided to embrace the nutritional recommendations wholeheartedly. Her strength and health have been steadily returning, and she is now able to resume some chemotherapy again.

Biofeedback and Self-Regulation: Proving It to Yourself

Another powerful source of messages to the body and to the unconscious belief structure is biofeedback for self-regulation. It is really only the self-regulation that is important, but biofeedback provides the convincing proof, to the cortex and to the unconscious, that control is indeed taking place. It is an undeniable, experienced fact that control is possible, that control is happening. It eliminates those doubts that can interfere with performance, that act as *counter-instructions* to the lower brain centers that direct our physical behavior. This is true of both inner and outer performance.

The following story, which appeared in local newspapers, is fascinating in this regard. Charles Garfield, who was an assistant clinical professor of medical psychology at the University of California in San Francisco, did a lecture tour in Europe. He lectured on his research on individuals who have survived usually-fatal cancers. This research was the subject of his award-winning book *Stress and Survival*. According to this research, one of the key things which survivors all had in common was a practice of frequently imagining that they were getting well. They envisioned that their tumors were decreasing in size.

Garfield was informed by Russian scientists that they were employing the same methods to help world-class athletes improve their performance. They use intensive—and intentional—mental imagery of desired outcomes. Garfield reported that the Russians have been researching mental imagery to enhance performance. In one major study, world-class athletes in speed skating, as well as in other sports, were divided into four groups. One group continued with physical training, one group spent one-fourth of its time on mental training and three-fourths in physical training, one group spent half its training time on each type of training, and the fourth group spent three-fourths of its time on mental training and only one-fourth on physical training.

At the next trials for the Olympics, athletes in the fourth group scored highest in performance and showed the most improvement. The next best was the group who spent half its time in mental training, and the worst group was the group that spent all its time in physical training. Around the world, in almost every country, the role of mental imagery in physical excellence is being recognized.

In fact, although it is not generally so conscious and deliberate and extensive, *all* of our physical activity is initiated by mental imagery. Learning a skill consists of image, action, feedback. Practice of a skill consists of repeating a performance until the feedback shows us that the action matches the imagery. This is obvious in the case of skills like shooting baskets, where the feedback is visual information about where the ball goes. But the conscious parts are still the intent or image—of where we want the ball to go—and the feedback—what actually happens. All the complex neuromuscular activities, from the motor cortex through spinal ganglions to motor fibers and flexor and extensor muscles, are not consciously directed.

It is becoming clear that control of many internal body processes is just as easy to learn as riding a bike or shooting baskets. Traditionally, the nervous system has been separated into two major divisions. One division, the "voluntary" nervous system, operates striate muscles like the muscles in our arms and legs, sometimes called the "voluntary" muscles, which we associate with conscious control. The other part of the nervous system has been called the "involuntary" nervous system, operating smooth muscles like those in the stomach, intestines, and blood vessels, generally thought of as operating totally unconsciously and involuntarily. It certainly *can* operate unconsciously and involuntarily, and usually does.

We have long known that the smooth muscles of heart, stomach, and intestines have responded to thoughts and emotions (thinking of something terrible leading to fear leading to vascular and intestinal responses.) Biofeedback is showing that these same smooth muscles also respond to *volition* and *images*. Biofeedback is making this knowledge and these abilities accessible to everybody, and biofeedback is making conscious control of the unconscious scientific, measurable, and verifiable.

Building A Personal Biofeedback Program

People have learned self-regulation of their physiology on their own for centuries. For most people, seeing is believing. Biofeedback gives experiential knowledge that the automatic parts of the body are in fact controllable. This knowledge—that the body can learn to show an immediate response to the mind—is as important in healing as the actual body changes that are brought about, such as reductions in tension and pain.

While it is theoretically possible to learn these skills without instrument-amplified biofeedback, it is difficult. It takes more time and more concentrated attention than most people are willing or able to give. On the other hand, these skills are easily learned with the help of a biofeedback therapist. Biofeedback is now available in most places in the country. The biofeedback therapist need not know anything about cancer treatment to help a cancer patient learn relaxation and self-regulation skills. The physiologic criteria that are most helpful are to be able to warm hands to ninety-six degrees Fahrenheit, to warm feet to ninety-three degrees Fahrenheit, and to relax muscles deeply.

Your physician may be able to help you locate a biofeedback therapist either from personal knowledge or from the National Register of Health Care Providers. If possible, find someone who is personally able to do these things. Biofeedback therapists who have mastered the skills themselves are the most effective and know from the inside the feelings of autonomic self-regulation and the requirements for instant relaxation.

Consciously directing our images and visualizations is the most important factor in self-healing. It is important that we each create our own visualizations, fitting our own conscious—*and unconscious*—understanding of what is occurring inside of our bodies. An active technique of visualization and imagery is first used to bring forth into consciousness elements previously not recognized or not accepted by the imager. This is a good opportunity for the repressed fears to express themselves, so that they can be dealt with. We need to deal in imagination with the negative aspects, as in psychosynthesis. If we begin with positive visualization, before discovering what we perceive the present situation to be, we are not dealing therapeutically with the situation.

What is needed next, with the help of others, is a clear explanation and understanding of the present condition; a clear, subjective sense of healthy internal processes; and a clear visualization, either symbolic or concrete, of the immune system overcoming cancer. The cancer cells are weak, confused, and disorganized, whereas the white cells and all the immune system elements are strong and powerful and are in tune with nature.

Incorporate your medical treatment into your visualization. Again, it is helpful to have an explanation and an understanding of how the treatment will ideally affect the body. If you are receiving chemotherapy, welcome it into your body as a powerful anti-cancer agent, the most powerful and the most specific for your type of cancer that can be found. It is an aid to your body in fighting cancer cells. Visualize the chemicals killing cancer cells and your body's healthy cells being strong and resistive, with a powerful capacity to repair any damage.

In radiation therapy, you can visualize all your healthy cells being resistive and reflective like little mirrors, directing the radiation onto the cancer. Visualize all your healthy cells along with all the healthy organs and tissues and systems of your body, cooperating to help resist and fight cancer.

Developing a Winning Visualization

In developing a visualization, trust your unconscious to inform you. As you become more and more responsive to your body, your body will become more and more responsive to you. Keep working until you have a winning visualization in which your white cells are victorious and your cancer is completely defeated.

There is a healing visualization that I use as a starting point. It is a very general visualization appropriate for everyone, at once a body scanning and a reminder of natural body processes. Put yourself in a comfortable, relaxed position. Let your body become quiet. Let your emotions become quiet. Let your mind become still. Be aware of your body touching the chair or bed, the position of your limbs, the expression on your face. Relax your face, your forehead, eyelids and jaws. Be aware of your breath. Think about your hands and feet being relaxed and warm.

Gently think about your vascular system, your entire blood stream from head to toe, including the arteries and arterioles and capillaries, the venules and veins. The blood stream is the transportation system for the body. It carries oxygen and nutriments and white cells to every living cell in the body, and it carries away the by-products of cell nutrition, carbon dioxide, and all the waste products of the body. Feel your blood surging right out to your fingertips and toes, to all your organs and tissues, to all your nerves and muscles, to all parts of your body.

Be aware, once again, of your breathing. Feel the blood surging into all the vessels in your lungs, and feel the fresh air and oxygen filling your lungs as you inhale. Imagine the oxygen and the blood meeting, the hemoglobin in your blood picking up the oxygen and carrying it to every cell in your body, right down to your toes. Imagine all your organs and muscles and tissues soaking up the oxygen as you inhale and giving up carbon dioxide and waste products as you exhale. Oxygen is a catalyst for metabolism in the cells, and every healthy living cell must have oxygen to live. Imagine all your cells soaking up the oxygen, being eager to receive it. Now think of the part of your body to which you would like to give extra attention. As you inhale, visualize and feel this part filling with oxygen. Imagine sending maximum circulation and oxygen and white cells and all the necessary nutriments and immune resources to it. Now you can simplify the image, and as you exhale, feel fatigue, pain, and tension flowing out of the body together with carbon dioxide and other waste products. Feel your body drawing in energy and healing, dispelling weakness, discomfort, and illness.

At this point, I often like to include a sense of connection with the entire planet and all living things. Think of the planet as a giant terrarium, floating in space, covered with its precious layer of atmosphere. The oxygen we breathe is provided by the plants, by all the trees and bushes and grasses and flowers on the planet. In return, the carbon dioxide we exhale is used by the plants in photosynthesis to make the green leaves and food and flowers that the plants provide. Oxygen is exhaled by the plants as a by-product of photosynthesis, or plant metabolism, and used by all the animal life on the planet in their growth and metabolism. Thus we are engaged in a breathing cycle with all the life on earth—the plants and the animal life, we and the plants—each getting from the other what we need to live and providing for each other simultaneously. For a moment, imagine the whole planet engaged in this breathing cycle as you breathe in and out, receiving and giving.

Imagine that you are lying in the sunlight. Visualize this sunlight as permeating every cell of your body. Imagine your body being transparent to sunlight, so that every cell, every organ and tissue and blood vessel and nerve and muscle in your whole body is filled with sunlight, each cell holding a little drop of sunlight, like a crystal or prism. As you inhale, imagine that the oxygen and the light combine, sparkling in a rainbow of color. Imagine inhaling light and energy with every inhalation and exhaling darkness, anxiety, agitation or depression with every exhalation. Feel calm energy and light coming in and darkness flowing out.

Now, turn your attention to the part of the body that you are especially working on, and see it permeated by sunlight. See every cell filled with sunlight and the sparkling rainbow colors as you inhale and the oxygen and light mingle. Feel a healing, a tingling and energized feeling of well-being in that part and in your whole body. Look down inside your being with a sense of benign regard and gratitude for all the good things your body has done for you all your life. Feel a sense of partnership with your body, a sense of mutual responsiveness. Repeat to yourself: "The more responsive I am to my body, the more responsive my body is to me."

Only one who has risked the fight with the dragon and is not overcome by it wins the hoard, the "treasure hard to attain." He alone has a genuine claim to self-confidence, for he has faced the dark ground of his self and thereby gained himself . . . He has arrived at an inner certainty which makes him capable of self-reliance.

—C. G. JUNG

What we nurture in ourselves will grow; that is nature's eternal law.

—GOETHE

CHAPTER SEVEN

Why Me?
Discovering the
Meaning

*O*ne of the most powerful of human needs is for our life to have meaning. Both psychological and physical illness can result when we fail to make sense of our lives or experiences, or when we experience the loss of persons or belief systems that give a meaning to our life. Conversely, the advent of serious illness can put new meaning into the context of our personal life. This is the essense of the existential question, "Why Me?"

"Why Me?" often starts out as a cry of outrage—why was I chosen, "like off a map or something," to suffer this? But as with Garrett's story, the others in this book, and so many other stories of self-responsibility, self-actualization in healing, "Why Me?" can end up with—"because I made something of it, because I learned something, because I could do it, because I worked for it!" Healing the self is a creative act that gives new meaning to life, to the process of life and living, and also to death, which is an inextricable part of life. Finding new meanings is a creative experience that in itself leads to healing.

Re-examining the Mind/Body Relationship

Our conceptual images of the nature of physical reality, the nature of the universe, and our images of human nature and human potential are undergoing rapid change. The images we hold of ourselves tend to become *actualized*, psychologically in the self-fulfilling prophecy, and physiologically in the biological consequences of beliefs. The emerging science of consciousness makes more credible the brain/mind/behavior influences on psychophysiology and highlights the very close links between state of mind and state of body. And the emerging science of psychoneuroimmunology, or neuroimmunomodulation, is already beginning to illuminate some of the biological mechanisms whereby this occurs.

Anatomical and functional pathways between the central nervous system and the immune system have been demonstrated. These suggest the mechanisms whereby brain, mind, and behavior can influence resistance to cancer. The work described in this book represents only a fraction of the psychological and behavioral treatments designed to enhance self-regulation of immune function. Psychological treatment of cancer has been widely reported. Alastair Cunningham has written a review of psychotherapy for cancer which consists of clinical studies indicating that psychological interventions may increase the longevity of cancer patients. He points out that these clinical investigations are methodologically weak because they have not been controlled, which critics point out to avoid the "type I" statistical error of accepting as true what has not been statistically proven. But Cunningham is careful to warn: "The danger, however, is that preoccupation with methodological exactitude may force us into an even more serious 'type II' error—dismissing as unfounded what may in fact be both true and very important. This danger seems to me to exist not only in mind and cancer, but across the whole subject of the effects of mind on physical disease." He points out that the results reported from the clinical treatment studies are *consistent* with each other and also are consistent with prospective studies on personality and cancer and on human stress and cancer, as well as with animal studies investigating the effects of applied stress on tumor growth.

Observations and single-case studies are an important means of increasing our knowledge, and as they accumulate, they are compelling in their weight of evidence. Now it is time to move beyond this stage to controlled experimental studies of specific ways in which the mind influences immune competence and of specific immunological changes associated with relaxation, with self-regulation of physiological processes, and with imagery and visualization.

Increasing interest among medical scientists in this emerging field prompted the National Institute of Health to sponsor the First International Conference on Neuroimmunomodulation in November of 1984. Much exciting research on numerous physical and chemical connections between the brain and the immune system, done at some of the most prestigious universities and hospitals from coast to coast, was reported, pointing the way for psychoneuroimmunology to become mainstream immunology, according to University of Rochester immunologist Nicholas Cohen.

According to a report by Sally Squires of the *Washington Post,* more than one hundred scientists from around the world took part in this four-day conference, including three American Nobel Prize winners: molecular biologist Marshall Nirenberg, Daniel Carleton Gajdusek, and Julius Axelrod, awarded a Nobel prize in medicine for his work on brain transmitters. Axelrod is now studying stress hormones and notes that the nervous system and the immune system have a lot in common and that a person under stress releases hormones that depress the nervous system.

The report further states that what attracts scientists is that since the immune system can be depressed, there may be ways it can be boosted; and if it can be boosted, scientists may one day be able to control it altogether, which would be an important step in conquering a host of illnesses from cancer to the common cold.

But since there are things that *we* do and ways *we* react to stress that can depress the immune system, there are things we can do *now* and ways we can learn to react *now* that can boost our own immune systems. *This is the good news.* As Elmer Green has stated, if we can make ourselves sick, then *obviously* we can make ourselves well; if there is such a thing as psychosomatic disease, then *obviously* there is such a thing as psychosomatic health. And that is what we can be working toward.

The Human Potential for Self-healing

In his book, *The Vital Balance,* Dr. Karl Menninger, one of the founders of The Menninger Foundation and one of the world's foremost psychiatrists, has said ". . . a broad reappraisal of the health-illness continuum . . . has implications for the goals of treatment. These need no longer be confined to a reinstatement of the *status quo ante* . . . but might push forward toward the development of new potentialities and transcendence of previous levels of vital balance to a state of being 'weller than well.' "

He asks if the aspiration to improve oneself—to become "weller than well—to reach out constantly toward a more perfect way of life—is a virtue and the blessing of only a few fortunate ones? Is it given only to geniuses, or is it something latent in all of us?"

And then Dr. Menninger asks a question of his reading audience that we might each want to ask of ourselves: "Should we be hesitant to contribute to world thinking what we know of human nature?" Alyce Green has modified that question slightly and has asked, "Should we be hesitant to contribute to world thinking what we know of human potential?" That is, the human potential to be well, the human potential for choice, for self-healing, self-direction, self-mastery—the human potential to be whole, physically, emotionally, mentally, and spiritually.

A physical medicine approach and a psychological approach to treatment taken together have more than an additive effect, just as the whole is more than the sum of its parts. Synergistically, anything done to help the physical body gain strength and feel better also helps the mind and mental attitude, and also anything done to improve mental attitude, mood, and beliefs has a beneficial effect upon the body.

In examining personality factors and cancer, there are two issues: personality factors affecting cancer *incidence;* and personality factors affecting cancer *survival* and *recovery.* Although the connection between personality and the etiology of cancer is of theoretical interest and will eventually have impact on prevention of cancer, in clinical treatment we are not so interested in questions of "how did we get here" as we are in "where do we go from here."

Clearly Understanding the Role of Denial

In working with patients and talking with many professionals, it has become increasingly obvious to me that we need to re-examine and clarify our concepts regarding the role of *denial* in cancer psychophysiology. Most investigators of personality and cancer agree that the common characteristics associated with cancer include repression and denial. On the other hand, paradoxically, denial is frequently cited as one of the primary characteristics of cancer survivors. In all of my experience, on closer examination, what is being called denial in the case of survivors is not a failure to recognize or perceive reality or the reality of their illness and the statistical probability of death, but rather it is a recognition that there are other possibilities and a willingness to work for a desirable outcome without any guarantees.

A positive attitude, which contributes so much biologically as well as psychologically to a person's well being, is often misperceived by many colleagues as denial. On the other hand, the concept of a positive attitude being helpful has been a source of confusion to many patients. If patients are inclined toward denial, they can and do continue to use denial, masquerading as a positive attitude. And many of the people I have worked with who have cancer have been afraid to confront reality for fear that they are then failing to be positive.

It is important that this be clear. It is not positive to say, "I am not hurting," in the face of pain; it is not positive to say, "I do not have a tumor," when the tumor is there; these are negative statements, particularly when they are false-to-fact. It sets up a dissonance between conscious and unconscious message when we try to tell ourselves things that are not true. We are aware, at least unconsciously, of our condition, and we are not really fooled when we are not told, or refuse to tell ourselves, the facts. Too much psychological energy gets used up in maintaining the fiction.

The most helpful attitude for healing is the most *realistic* appraisal of what *is* and the most *optimistic* appraisal of what *can be*. Denial is employed when we deny the truth, and truth pertains to what is. Probabilities are not truth, they are just probabilities.

The realization of this comes as a big relief to patients who have been trying hard to keep a positive attitude and confusing that with a "rose-colored glasses" attitude that refuses to acknowledge any unpleasant reality. We cannot confront and deal with what we refuse to acknowledge. In order to visualize our immune system destroying our tumor or cancer cells, it is necessary to have some sort of image of the problem; in order to relax when we are tense, we must first develop an awareness of tension as it arises. The first step in gaining voluntary control of internal states is *awareness*. Knowledge empowers us, and the more knowledge we have of our internal state (not necessarily technical knowledge, but acknowledgment), the better able we are to impact and influence its processes.

The Quality of Life:
Not How Much but How Good

Once when Garrett was on a program with Dr. Gerald Jampolsky in Kansas City, Jerry asked Garrett how many times he needed to practice his visualizations. Garrett was always a diligent and enthusiastic practicer, and I was confident that he would reply that he practiced every day. But Garrett was silent for a moment and then responded strongly, "It isn't how *much* that matters, it's how *good!*" I think this is a deep truth, a truth that pertains to everything we seek after, and that can be applied to life itself. It isn't how much that matters, but how good.

REFERENCES

Achterberg, Jeanne, and G. Frank Lawlis. *Imagery of Cancer.* Champaign, Illinois: Institute for Personality and Ability Testing, 1978.

Achterberg, Jeanne, and G. Frank Lawlis. *Bridges of the Bodymind.* Champaign, Illinois: Institute for Personality and Ability Testing, 1980.

Ader, Robert, and N. Cohen. Behaviorally conditioned immunosuppression. *Psychosomatic Medicine* 37 (1975): 333-340.

Ader, Robert. *Psychoneuroimmunology.* New York: Academic Press, 1981.

Appelbaum, Stephen A. *Out in Inner Space.* Garden City, New York: Anchor Press/Doubleday, 1979.

Assagioli, Roberto. *Psychosynthesis.* New York: Viking Press, 1971.

Assagioli, Roberto. *The Act of Will.* New York: Viking Press, 1973.

Bahnson, C. B., and M. G. Bahnson. Denial and repression of primitive impulses and of disturbing emotions in patients with malignant neoplasms. In D. M. Kissen and L. LeShan, eds. *Psychosomatic Aspects of Neoplastic Disease.* Philadelphia: Lippincott, 1964.

Bahnson, C. B., and D. M. Kissen, eds. *Psychophysiological Aspects of Cancer,* Annals of the New York Academy of Sciences. 125 (1966): 773-1055.

Bahnson, C. B. Stress and cancer: the state of the art. *Psychosomatics* 22, 3 (1981): 207-220.

Barofsky, I. Issues and approaches to the psychosocial assessment of the cancer patient. In C. K. Prokip and L. A. Bradley, eds. *Medical Psychology: Contributions to Behavioral Medicine.* New York: Viking Press, 1981.

Boyd, Doug. *Rolling Thunder.* New York: Random House, 1974.

Borysenko, J. Z. Behavioral-physiological factors in the development and management of cancer. *General Hospital Psychiatry* 4 (1982): 69-74.

Burish, T. G., and J. N. Lyles. Effectiveness of relaxation training in reducing adverse reactions to cancer chemotherapy. *Journal of Behavioral Medicine* 4 (1981): 65-78.

Cade, C. Maxwell, and Nona Coxhead. *The Awakened Mind.* New York: Delacorte Press, 1979.

Chandra, R. K. *The Immunology of Nutritional Disorders.* Chicago: Medical Yearbook Publishers, 1980.

Children of the Center for Attitudinal Healing. *There is a Rainbow Behind Every Dark Cloud.* Millbrae, California: Celestial Arts Publishing, 1978.

Cousins, Norman, Guest Editorial: Cancer and Placebos. *CA-A Cancer Journal for Clinicians* No. 2 (April/March, 1981): 31.

Cunningham, A. J. Psychotherapy for cancer. A review. *Advances,* Institute for the Advancement of Health 1, (1981): 8-14.

Day, Stacy B., ed. *Readings in Oncology.* American Institute of Stress and The International Foundation of Biosocial Development and Human Health. New York: 1980.

Derogatis, L. R., M. D. Abeloff and N. Melisaratos. Psychological coping mechanisms and survival time in metastatic breast cancer. *Journal of the American Medical Association* 242 (1979): 1504-1507.

Gabbard, G., and S. Twemlow. *With the Eyes of the Mind: An Empirical Analysis of Out-of-Body-States.* New York: Praeger, 1984.

Garfield, C. *Stress and Survival.* St. Louis, Missouri: C. B. Mosby, 1979.

Gerson, Max. *A Cancer Therapy: Results of Fifty Cases.* Del Mar, California: Totality Books, 1977.

Green, Elmer. Psychophysiologic Correlates of Expectancy. Presidential Address, Biofeedback Society of America. San Diego, 1979.

Green, E., and A. Green. *Beyond Biofeedback.* New York: Delacorte Press, 1977.

Green, E., A. Green and E. D. Walters. Voluntary control of internal states: Psychological and physiological. *Journal of Transpersonal Psychology* II (1970): 1-26.

Greer, S., and P. M. Silberfarb. Psychological concomitants of cancer: Current state of research. *Psychological Medicine* 12 (1972): 563-573.

Groff, S., and J. Halifax. *The Human Encounter with Death.* New York: Dutton, 1977.

Hall, Howard, Santo Longo, and Richard Dixon. Hypnosis and the immune system: The effect of hypnosis on T and B cell function. Paper presented to the Society for Clinical and Experimental Hypnosis, 33rd Annual Meeting. Portland, Oregon: October, 1981.

Holden, C. Cancer and the mind: How are they connected? *Science* 200 (1978): 1363-1369.

Holt, Robert. Imagery: The return of the ostracized. *American Psychologist* 19 (1964): 254-264.

Horowitz, Mardi. *Image Formation and Cognition.* New York: Appleton-Century-Crofts, 1970.

Hutschnecker, A. A. *The Will to Live.* New York: Prentice Hall, 1951.

Jacobs, J. S. Cancer: Host resistance and host acquiescence. In J. A. Gengerelli and F. J. Kirkner, eds. *Psychological Variables in Human Cancer: A Symposium* Berkeley, California: University of California Press, 1954.

Jampolsky, G. *Love is Letting Go of Fear.* Berkeley, California: Celestial Arts, 1979.

References

Kelley, W. D. *One Answer to Cancer.* Beverly Hills, California: International Association of Cancer Victors and Friends, 1974.

Kissen, D. M. and L. LeShan, eds. *Psychosomatic Aspects of Neoplastic Disease.* Philadelphia: Lippincott, 1964.

Klopfer, B. Psychological variables in human cancer. *Journal of Projective Techniques* 21 (1957): 331-340.

Kohut, Heinz. *The Restoration of the Self.* New York: International Universities Press, 1977.

Kübler-Ross, Elisabeth. *On Death and Dying.* New York: Macmillan, 1969.

Kutz, I., J. Z. Borysenko and Herbert Benson. Meditation and psychotherapy: A rationale for the integration of dynamic psychotherapy, the relaxation response, and mindfulness meditation. *The American Journal of Psychiatry* 142 (1985): 1-8.

Landau, R. L. and J. M. Gustafson. Death is not the enemy. *Journal of the American Medical Association* 252 (1984): 2458.

LeShan, L. An emotional life history pattern associated with neoplastic disease. *Annals of the New York Academy of Science* 125 (1966): 780-793.

LeShan, L. Psychological states as factors in the development of malignant disease: A critical review. *Journal of the National Cancer Institute* 22 (1959): 1-18.

LeShan, L. *You Can Fight For Your Life: Emotional Factors in The Causation of Cancer.* New York: M. Evans & Company, 1977.

Lewin, R. *In Defense of the Body: An Introduction to the New Immunology.* Garden City, New York: Anchor Press/Doubleday, 1974.

Lockart, R. A. *Cancer in Myth and Dream: An Exploration into the Archetypal Relation Between Dreams and Disease.* Spring Publications, Zurich.

Locke, S. E. Stress, adaptation and immunity: Studies in humans. *General Hospital Psychiatry* 4 (1982): 49-58.

Locke, S. E., and M. Hornig-Rohan, eds. *Mind and Immunity: Behavioral Immunology, An Annotated Bibliography, 1976-1982.* Institute for the Advancement of Health, 1983.

Menninger, Karl. *The Vital Balance.* New York: Viking Press, 1963.

Milner, L. S. Behavioral techniques and oncology: How to alleviate chemotherapeutic reactions through endomeditation. *Behavioral Medicine* 8 (1981). 26-28.

Moler, G., and E. Moler. The concept of immunological surveillance against neoplasia. *Transplant* 28 (1976): 3-16.

Moody, Raymond. *Life After Life.* St. Simons Island, Georgia: Mockingbird Books, 1975.

Morales, B. L. Eyesight—A barometer of health. *Let's Live* (June, 1981).

Murphy, Gardner. *Challenge of Psychical Research.* New York: Harper, 1961.

Neurenberg, Phil. *Freedom From Stress.* Honesdale, Pennsylvania: Himalaya Institute, 1981.

Norris, P. A., and S. L. Fahrion. Autogenic Biofeedback in Psychophysiological Therapy and Stress Management. In R. L. Woolfolk and P. M. Lehrer, eds. *Principles and Practice of Stress Management.* New York: The Guilford Press, 1984.

Pelletier, Kenneth R. *Mind as Healer, Mind as Slayer.* New York: Delacorte and Delta, 1977.

Pelletier, Kenneth R. *Holistic Medicine: From Stress to Optimum Health.* New York: Delacorte Press, 1979.

Peterson, L. G., M. K. Popkin and R. C. W. Hall. Psychiatric aspects of cancer. *Psychosomatics* 22 (1981): 774-793.

Pritikin, N., and P. M. McGrady, Jr. *The Pritikin Program for Diet and Exercise.* New York: Grosset & Dunlap, 1979.

Progoff, Ira. *The Death and Rebirth of Psychology.* New York: The Julian Press, 1956.

Progoff, Ira. *The Practice of Process Meditation.* New York: Dialogue House Library, 1980.

Rabkin, J. G., and E. L. Struening. Life events, stress, and illness. *Science* 194 (1976): 1013-1020.

Rasmussen, A. F., Jr. Emotions and immunity. *Annals of the New York Academy of Science* 164 (1969): 458-461.

Riley, V. Mouse mammary tumors: Alteration of incidence as apparent function of stress. *Science* 189 (1981): 465-467.

Riley, V. Psychoneuroendocrine influences of immunocompetence and neuroplasia. *Science* 212 (1981): 1100-1109.

Ring, Kenneth. *Life at Death.* New York: Coward, McCann & Geoghegan, 1980.

Rogers, M. P., D. Dubey and P. Reich. The influence of the psyche and the brain on immunity and disease susceptibility: A critical review. *Psychosomatic Medicine* 41 (1979): 147-164.

Rosch, P. J. Some thoughts on the endemiology of cancer. Chapter in *Readings in Oncology.* New York: International Foundation for Biosocial Development and Human Health, 1980.

Rosch, P. J. Stress and cancer: A disease of adaptation? In Jean Taché, Hans Selye and S. B. Day, eds. *Cancer, Stress and Death.* New York: Plenum, 1979.

Salsbury, K. H., and E. M. Johnson. *The Indispensable Cancer Handbook.* Washington, D.C.: Wideview Books, 1981.

Samuels, M., and N. Samuels. *Seeing With the Mind's Eye.* New York: Random House, 1975.

Simmons, Harold E. *The Psychogenic Biochemical Aspects of Cancer.* Sacramento, California: Psychogenic Disease Publishing Company, 1979.

Simonton, O. Carl, Stephanie Matthews-Simonton and James Creighton. *Getting Well Again: A Step-By-Step Self Help Guide to*

References

Overcoming Cancer for Patients and Their Families. Los Angeles: J. P. Tarcher, 1978.

Sklar, L. S., and H. Anisman. Social stress influences tumor growth. *Psychosomatic Medicine* 42 (1980): 347-365.

Solomon, G. F., A. A. Amkraut and P. Kaspar. Immunity, emotions and stress: With special reference to the mechanisms of stress effects on the immune system. *Annals of Clinical Research* 6 (1974): 313-322.

Solomon, G. F., A. A. Amkraut and R. T. Rubin. Stress and psychoimmunological response. In B. A. Stoll, ed. *Mind and Cancer Prognosis.* New York: John Wiley and Son, 1979.

Sperry, R. W. Changing priorities. *Annual Review of Neuroscience* 4 (1981): 1-15.

Stein, M. A biopsychosocial approach to immune function and medical disorders. *The Psychiatric Clinics of North America* 4 (1981): 203-223.

Stein, M., R. C. Schaivi and M. Camerino. Influences of brain and behavior on the immune system. *Science* 191 (1976): 435-440.

Stein, M. Stress, brain and immune function (Abstract). *The Gerontologist* 22 (1981): 203.

Stoll, B. A., ed. *Mind and Cancer Prognosis.* New York: John Wiley & Sons, 1979.

Squires, Sally. The mind fights back—Secrets of the immune system: Scientists study how smiles boost it and stress supresses it. *Washington Post Health,* January 9, 1985.

Thomas, C. B., K. R. Duszynski and J. W. Shaffer. Family attitudes reported in youth as potential predictors of cancer. *Psychosomatic Medicine* 41 (1979): 287, 302.

Thomas, Lewis. *The Medusa and the Snail.* New York: Viking Press, 1979.

Thomas, Lewis. *The Youngest Science: Notes of a Medicine-Watcher.* New York: Viking Press, 1979.

Taché, J., H. Selye and S. B. Day. *Cancer, Stress and Death.* New York: Plenum, 1979.

Weyer, E. M., ed. Psychophysiological Aspects of Cancer. *Annals of the New York Academy of Sciences* 125 (1966): 773-1055.

Woolsfolk, Robert L., and Paul M. Lehrer. *Principles and Practice of Stress Management.* New York: Guilford Press, 1984.

VIDEO MATERIALS

ABC Mind and Medicine series, Good Morning America, 1984.
NBC Donahue and Kids, Project Peacock series.